WILLIAM L. SACHS & MICHAEL S. BOS

FRAGMENTED LIVES

Finding Faith in an Age of Uncertainty

Morehouse Publishing
NEW YORK

Morehouse Publishing, 19 East 34th Street, New York, NY 10016
Morehouse Publishing is an imprint of Church Publishing Incorporated.
www.churchpublishing.org
Cover design by Laurie Klein Westhafer, Bounce Design
Typeset by Denise Hoff

Library of Congress Cataloging-in-Publication Data

Names: Sachs, William L., 1947- author.
Title: Fragmented lives : finding faith in an age of uncertainty /
  William L. Sachs and Michael S. Bos.
Description: New York : Morehouse Publishing, 2016. | Includes
  bibliographical references. | Description based on print version record
  and CIP data provided by publisher; resource not viewed.
Identifiers: LCCN 2016017649 (print) | LCCN 2016005611 (ebook) |
  ISBN 9780819232816 (ebook) | ISBN 9780819232809 (pbk.)
Subjects: LCSH: Faith. | Christianity and culture. | Trust in
  God--Christianity. | Non-church-affiliated people.
Classification: LCC BV4637 (print) | LCC BV4637 .S23 2016 (ebook) |
  DDC 234/.23--dc23
LC record available at https://lccn.loc.gov/2016017649

Printed in the United States of America

Contents

Why We Struggle

> Where life with God gets rich and provocative is
> when you dig into a tradition that you
> did not invent all for yourself.
>
> —Lillian Daniel

The Question of Faith Today

The climb had become exhilarating. Not everyone could accept the challenge of this steep western peak. But it was ideal for two friends accustomed to climbing together. The extent of their conditioning matched the strength of their friendship. They had scaled heights before and gathered a collection of memories that formed their bond. We could face anything together, Matt thought, for Brad was like a brother to him. There was complete faith in one another. They would always be there for each other, they regularly professed. But their faith would be tested.

The day Matt and Brad would always remember began with quiet excitement. Their goal was the top of a nine-thousand-foot peak. In a few hours they would be there. Breaking camp they set out in moderate temperatures with a slight breeze. A clear trail led upward from the campsite. Indeed everything seemed clear. Nothing stood in their way. No clouds obscured the path or their friendship. They could do anything together, or so it seemed on a clear morning. The beauty that loomed in fresh daylight confirmed every hope.

That beauty became stark as trees receded and then ended. Above the tree line there were no shadows, only dramatic, infinite views. They were making this climb together, and that feeling would only deepen, each assumed. Long imagined and carefully mapped, the climb was going flawlessly. Already each was thinking of further adventures; after this climb they could surely do anything they chose. Only faithful friends could scale such heights. The sky was the limit, and now Matt and Brad were about to touch it.

Who hasn't had such a moment with a treasured friend? Who hasn't felt surges of possibility with someone? Who hasn't experienced moments of complete faith and assurance? The mountain could be a metaphor. Everyone, at some moment or other, believes something daring is possible, with someone else, perhaps in nature. Nothing can get in the way; anything is possible, there for the choosing. That moment had come for Matt and Brad. Together they were doing it, each feeling triumphant, marveling at the scenery as they climbed. It was dramatic and breathtaking. Even the flashes of lightning in the distance added a dimension of beauty. Matt and Brad admired the brilliant show of power as they neared the summit.

Nestled in the feeling of conquering this peak together, Matt and Brad were slow to grasp that nature's power was enveloping them. The distant clouds and flashes were no longer so distant. Later each recalled that it suddenly seemed dark, with ominous rumbles. Above the trees, near the summit, images of touching the sky lost their appeal. Now the sky could easily seize them and it would not be pretty. They were atop a natural lightning arrester, vulnerable, terribly at risk. Suddenly confidence shattered. At once hesitant, they now saw little but darkness punctuated by blinding flashes and loud explosions.

Then, as if struck by lightning, Matt realized he was alone. It happened in an instant, he later realized, though at the time it seemed like slow motion. In the midst of sudden, roaring darkness, Brad was gone. One moment they were together, their bond secure, on the verge of conquest. Then swallowed in fiery gloom, Brad had vanished and Matt was forced to regroup. Trying to make sense of what happened, he finally glimpsed Brad, now distant, running rapidly down the path away from him. Already so far gone that Matt needed the lightning flashes, like brief spotlights, to glimpse Brad's back moving hastily away. In his fright, it seemed Brad might stumble. But he plunged on, leaving Matt alone.

Briefly Matt studied Brad's retreat with abstract fascination. But a lightning crash nearby punctured his reflection, and drenching rains completed his awakening. As if shaken from sleep, now muttering in anger, Matt began his own descent. He was stunned that nature had so quickly become a dangerous adversary. Even more he was numb that friendship, with all the hopes invested in it, had been abandoned so abruptly. Without a word of warning Brad had run away, leaving Matt alone.

In what can you believe? Who or what do you trust? In a word, is it possible to find faith? No questions are more avidly pursued today than these. As old forms of faith, and the religious institutions that propound them, are questioned, more people are striking out on their own to find faith for themselves. The typical places to look are in the natural world around us, and in people with whom we might share the journey. Often the results are dramatic. A young woman on a youth pilgrimage reflected on the sense of finding God while on a group expedition to the California coast:

> While on this trip I have discovered that I find God in nature. In the tumbling hills of golden brown, the vast magnolia trees, the rushing creeks, the sparkling ocean at sunset, and the lush greenery in the woods I feel God's presence. In the serenity and beauty of the world around me I find peace and comfort. God wraps around me like a blanket, surrounding me in his overwhelming love.
>
> Perhaps it's the incredible people around me or the close proximity of the California coast, but while on this pilgrimage I have been able to reach out to God in ways I haven't been able to before. I look to the field of stars, feel the brisk wind, or gaze upon the earth around me, and think of the words, "Be still and know that I am God" while taking deep breaths. The effect is a quiet mind full of love and reflection.

In such an experience, faith seemingly finds us. The sense of oneness with nature and with other people infuses hope and possibility. Who needs anything else, one wonders in such a moment? We have found God directly, personally, and yet together. The moment is magic.

Faith Drift: Moving Away from Religion

Increasing numbers of people find such transcendent moments make religion and religious institutions irrelevant. At best, religion gets in the way. At worst, religion distorts the goodness that can readily be ours, or so many people conclude. We have come to think of religion as that which requires us to believe certain things, whether we believe they are true or not, and to do certain things, whether we think they are good for us or not.

In research that professor of social work Brené Brown has done, she discovered that when women speak of religious experiences of shame they use the terms "church" and "religion." And when they speak of spiritual resilience, they use "faith" and "spirituality."[1] People are distancing themselves from religion and its purveyor, the church. Instead we describe ourselves as being "spiritual but not religious" or wanting "spirituality without structure." But what does all of this mean?

It means that many of us are experiencing faith drift. We sense a spiritual longing within us, but we are not sure what to do with it or where it may take us. This longing seeks connection with others, and yes, maybe even participation in an "organized religion." But we don't know where to turn or what or whom to trust on this journey.

If this is how you are feeling, we want you to know that you are not alone. We are living in an age of uncertainty and confusion about who or what we can trust. Finding faith in such a time is our greatest challenge.

Yet faith itself is fragmented. With the rise of religious and cultural diversity, we share fewer and fewer values, beliefs, ideals, norms, and rituals that bind us together as a community. Instead, we have fragments of our lives that connect in different ways with different people in different places. We are constantly adapting and adopting new ways of being to fit whatever context we may find ourselves in.

> Our society is so fragmented, our family lives
>   so sundered by physical and emotional distance,
> our friendships so sporadic,
> our intimacies so "in-between" things
>   and often so utilitarian,
> that there are few places where we can feel truly safe.
>
> —Henri J. M. Nouwen,
> *Life of the Beloved: Spiritual Living in a Secular World*

This is compounded by the way we receive fragmented information. As we watch the news we learn of refugees fleeing a war-torn country, a heat wave hitting California, a dog that skateboards, opposition to a new Walmart being built, the latest scores for baseball, a drug that helps erectile dysfunction, and another candidate entering the presidential race. As James Davison Hunter observes, the electronic media is able to inundate us rapidly and intensely with news that "compartmentalizes the world and places its parts together in incoherent ways."[2] We have no larger narrative into which to fit these fragments of information to make sense of it all.

Our attention spans have become fragmented. We now practice "continuous partial attention." Our lives are filled with disruptions and distractions as constant phone alerts inform us of a new tweet, text, Facebook post or Snapchat. When we're out with friends, our phones are ready at our sides so we can keep conversations going with our friends "out there" while being physically present (kind of) with other friends. We pride ourselves on our ability to multitask and thumb type with blazing speed. Yet the truth is that our attention is less focused, we make more mistakes, and we have little time to ponder the larger, more important matters in life.

We have come to accept the fragmented nature of life as part of the modern condition, and in so doing, we take on the stress and frantic pace of life that comes with it. We sense that we're always chasing something and going somewhere, but we're never sure what that something is and where that somewhere will take us.

Finding Faith in an Age of Confusion

It is probably no surprise that two pastors are going to suggest that faith is what is missing amidst the fragmented, confusing times in which we live. But when we speak of faith, we are speaking of something that is larger than religion itself. James Fowler, a pioneer in understanding faith formation, describes it this way: "Prior to our being religious or irreligious . . . we are already engaged with issues of faith. Whether we become nonbelievers, agnostics or atheists, we are concerned with how to put our lives together and with what will make life worth living."[3]

Because of the changes in culture we have mentioned, we must rethink and reframe the possibilities for faith today. Faith is the pathway to find meaning, wholeness, and significance. Faith isn't just about beliefs and doctrines. It is about a way of seeing and living in the world that allows us to flourish in it. Like the psalmist, we all dream of the day when we will "flourish like the palm tree, and grow like a cedar in Lebanon. They are planted in the house of the LORD; they flourish in the courts of our God" (Ps. 92:12–13).

Though we glimpse it incompletely, the goal of our journeys is to find faith. At first we are unsure, and even resist the thought that this is about "God." That can sound like someone else's answers for questions we are asking. But we want something basic, to ground our efforts, a reality that seems far away. We want to climb it, map it, make it our own. Thus our questions multiply. Who can you trust? What gives your life meaning? Where can you find people with whom to journey? Who will you become? Much is waiting to be discovered. But what will come of it? As the questions multiply they become intense. Our lives are fragmented among hopes and fears, bits of friendships and belonging, gaps of loneliness and uncertainty. In the midst of our fragmentation we seek faith. But what do faith, and our search for it, mean?

In this book we describe the meaning of faith. This old word is acquiring new meaning, inspiring new efforts, spilling over previous limits that restricted it. Faith is about who you are and how you live; what you seek and with whom. Faith requires trust in people, experiences, and ideas. On this basis we build connections to the world around us. Through the lens of faith we interpret what happens as good or bad, ominous or hopeful. By faith we organize our lives, dare to speak, or choose to be silent. By faith we set priorities, give our time and energy, indeed invest our emotional selves. As much as what and how, faith is the "why" that animates our lives.

On most good days, our faith does not come into question. We plunge ahead with assurance. But there seem to be fewer such times for many people; our ability to have faith has been shaken. Nature has turned cloudy. People have let us down. Business and government and even the church have shown their clay feet. Faith is in short supply and our hesitation to commit ourselves has grown. It is tempting for many people to treat faith as if it is an abstract question they can answer another day. But faith is the stuff of our lives. We reveal our faith, or lack thereof, by how we live. Every day we make choices, face situations, and reach crossroads. We struggle for the certainty faith promises. But what is faith? In what or whom can we trust?

Our search for faith centers on a hope of building a significant life, framed by an emphasis on our individualism and freedom to make choices. In chapter 1, we explain that this means being part of something worthwhile that is larger than ourselves. This longing can easily take destructive turns, for we are vulnerable. But the path toward a life of significance can unfold in healthy, mutually beneficial ways.

Chapter 2 links the search for significance with a readiness to discover wonder in the world, to be dazzled. Wonder is the basis of faith, for at its best wonder entails discovery of what had been near but not previously appreciated. St. Augustine observed that people gaze at the height of mountains and the waves of the sea, yet "they pass by themselves without wondering."[4] Wonder is a feeling that leads outward, beyond the limits of ourselves, toward connection. In this movement outward, faith takes root.

Movement is a key category, as chapter 3 describes. The most purposeful movement shapes us as pilgrims, intent on life as a journey toward a momentous destination. A rich way of life can unfold in new and unexpected ways. Faith becomes as much the progression as it does the destination. The journey toward it builds as it proceeds. In the process we find that we are walking together with others. In a world where so much seems impermanent, the journey toward faith gives us the bearings we need. No journey lacks effort or diversions and upheavals. The core issues of life, and of our own identities, surface fully. In the midst of these encounters, we find ourselves in the presence of God, that is, of a sense of ultimate power and possibility.

In chapter 4 we consider how we find the faith to live differently. At its heart is trust. Trust is not a passive state but a call to action, and we explore what it means to move into a deeper trust in God. This is what gives rise to our courage to live differently. It doesn't give any guarantee of how our future will unfold. But it gives us the confidence that our faith will help us navigate the choices and challenges we'll face, and the decisions we make will lead us to a life of significance.

We all have an innate yearning not only to live lives of significance, but to participate in things that last. In chapter 5 we consider what it means to be a part of that which is lasting and real, trusting that only then will we fully come alive. We also discover that faith is only alive and lasting when it is shared. In chapter 6 we urge that faith and the journey animating it must be put into action. Faith cannot be confined to private thoughts and feelings. Faith must spill over into our relations to the world, prompting service rooted in compassion. Faithful people strive to make the world a better place.

The implications are far-reaching. We seek to guide people who are trying to make sense of the life of faith for themselves. We also encourage congregations and their leaders to respond creatively to the variety of faith journeys today. People inside and outside the church need its ministries at their best. The meaning of being on a faith journey together is shifting, we conclude. What increasing numbers of people mean by faith, and how they are seeking it, are primary resources for building faith community today. The churches need the fresh energies of people in pursuit of faith.

Toward Formative Connection

> Now faith is the assurance of things hoped for,
> the conviction of things not seen.
>
> —Hebrews 11:1

Can today's spiritual longings and personal searches lead us to genuine faith? Is there a true alignment between the lives we are trying to build, revealed in the choices we make, and faith tradition, especially Christian faith, which we hold? Religion is the crux of the matter. Part of our task in this book is to sort out what religion and spirituality mean in terms of our pursuits of wholeness and direction. As we proceed with this narrative, the relation between religion and spirituality, traditions and the institutions that represent them, will become clear. For now, we can offer some initial thoughts on the nature of faith, as we seek it today:

- Faith involves active relations to people and to the world, including nature;

- Faith taps our hopes and awakens pursuit of destinations we cannot see but strain to reach;

- Faith entails encounters with unexpected realities, some harsh, and strains our desire to control ourselves and our circumstances;

- Faith may reside in symbolic objects representing experiences where our identity has become invested;

- Faith invites us to see aspects of life as sacred because of the power they hold for us.

By speaking in such terms, we begin to consider faith as religious, knowing that such a step is problematic for many people. But we will unfold a description of faith that defies how religion is often presumed to be. In religious terms, faith may be presumed to mean certainty, trust, unquestioned obedience, unshakeable foundations. Such a view of faith centers on dogmas that must be accepted whole, unchallenged. Tangibly such a view prompts images of institutions and authority figures that embody the unswerving assurance religion appears to require. Because of such images many people shun religion for the dynamism and individualism that promises life.

A certain appeal has surrounded the presumed meaning of faith. Certainty can draw people together with shared confidence. Though one might question only with difficulty, one need not puzzle over choices: there are few. Instead purpose and direction arise once one accepts the required beliefs and practices. A great deal of personal uncertainty becomes moot. One could presume one's salvation in the next life while resting secure in one's identity in this life.

While many people face perplexing life choices, others claim to have left choice behind because of their religious assurance. The appeal of fundamentalism is clear: it promises to reduce the range of life's uncertainty. However, we argue for religious tradition from a different perspective. We sense that rigid religious systems gloss over difficult, inevitable choices all of us face, sooner or later. Fundamentalist religion, rooted in literal, selective readings of sacred scriptures, glosses over the truth and richness of the faith traditions. We write as Christians, committed to the revelation of God in Jesus Christ. But we honor the major religions, with whom we have warm connections. We welcome the breadth of faith experience.

> Fanaticism is overcompensation for doubt.
>
> —Attributed to Robertson Davies

Regardless of the beliefs they hold, congregations and wider religious institutions of all sorts may not do justice to the faith search today. In their eagerness to offer answers, religious leaders and organizations may not appreciate the journeys people intend and the choices they are pursuing. Within the faith traditions are great stores of wisdom. Probed deeply and honestly, tradition comes alive, inviting us to locate our lives in abiding purpose and goodness. Tradition can also draw us toward one another in faith community, and toward caring response to need. This is how we will present Christianity; this is the true basis for the faith journey today.

How might the journey begin? Joshua rejected religion as an adolescent, passively resisting overtures at home and at school. At college, he maintained his resolute stance. His freedom to choose, and to reject, was resolute. But what, he slowly began to wonder, did he actually believe? The question haunted him until, as if by chance, he fell in with a group of people at a Unitarian congregation. Beliefs were of no immediate consequence to him, and among Unitarians few beliefs, other than spacious freedom, were apparent. More important, Joshua found a group of students like himself. Among them there was a spectrum of belief, with urgent questions for one person striking no resonance with another.

It was the asking of the questions together, then sharing meals, then going to movies, then talking half the night about life and faith and the whole gamut of undergraduate subjects. It was formative connection, a link to a group of people serious about life and each other. Through their tie to one another, and the aura of faith tradition, there was a sense of going somewhere, developing and growing. They had a great deal of fun; they also had soul-searching times of conversation and simply being with one another.

Joshua still was not certain about "God." There were many past assumptions to shed. But he had begun to touch something sacred, beyond what he had known before. He had also begun to feel the first inklings of faith, for himself, not dictated by someone else. His journey took shape, as many journeys do, in formative connections to others seeking direction amid all they faced. It can happen in a myriad of ways. Through such connections faith first comes into focus.

Joshua's experience is an important illustration. It reflects the experience of countless people of all generations today. In fact, it is an experience that recurs in various phases of one's life. When the journey we call life takes a new turn former assurances must be reframed. Joshua and other young adults become older. They experience gain and loss, hello and good-bye. They move, change jobs, trade old interests for new ones. They feel in control one moment, and out of control the next. They move between satisfaction, even elation, and anger and depression. In between, most days are mundane, without apparent direction. But somehow they sense that there is more to life and it is within reach.

This book is written for people of all ages who want to look beneath life's surface. Perhaps you find yourself asking questions that won't go away nor being satisfied by quick reactions or old assumptions. You find yourself wondering who and what to believe, and the hint of doubt further discomforts. You fear your life going off track and you try to keep going without complete success. Just when your life seemed clear and focused, an unexpected twist challenged what you believed was secure. You had to regroup, maybe even begin again.

We do not begin our description of faith with the obvious signposts of traditional religion or current spirituality. We begin with the inevitable twists and turns of personal experience. Amid the joys and despairs, obstacles and rewards, we perceive a way to live that unites our fragmented lives into substantial, purposeful journeys. How this can unfold is the path of our narrative. So let us turn now to follow the journey of faith as it begins.

Acknowledgments

The creation of a book resembles the search for faith in a fragmented life. At first, people and ideas flow past, without form, unfiltered, with little interruption. The challenge is to gain perspective and to discover patterns that shape meaning. Drilling below the surface is the task. It requires linking ideals of faith to instances of personal experience. Fortunately, we met a number of people who illustrated how faith can come alive in one's life, how reality and ideal can merge. The people with whom we spoke provided illustrative stories for this book. Even more, they provided encouragement when we could have faltered. Our conversation partners confirm that life is a quilt, given purpose and form by varied sources, all making faith come alive. They have given this book life.

We are especially grateful to Jack DeLoyht, Peter Johnson, Allison Seay, and Michael Sweeney.

Particular thanks are due to Allison Seay. She read much of the manuscript and offered helpful thoughts. A published poet, she brought interpretive perspectives that extended our insights. We are grateful for her interest.

Our various explorations in preparation of this book left one indelible impression: faith must begin inwardly and personally. Then, to mature and flourish, faith must move outwardly and become lived with one another. We hope this book will encourage faith as a journey that takes us out of ourselves individually and toward greater, shared commitment. In the midst of such a journey, God is vivid and loving. Only then can faith's promise come alive.

CHAPTER 1

Looking for Significance

Living Like Tantalus

In Greek mythology there is the story of Tantalus, also known as King Phrygian. Tantalus was a favored son of Zeus, and so Zeus invited Tantalus to Mount Olympus to dine with the gods and learn their secrets. This was truly a privilege to be cherished.

Unfortunately, Tantalus, wanting to enhance his position with the mortals below, would steal the favored food of the gods. He brought it back to the people to share with them while revealing the secrets of the gods. Obviously the people loved him for this, but the gods were not impressed. For this, as well as some other immoral acts, he was sent to the deepest pit of Hades for all of eternity.

The gods constructed a special kind of hell for Tantalus. He was placed in a pool of water with branches of luscious fruit hanging overhead. It doesn't sound bad, but here's the catch. Whenever he would bend down to get a drink from the pool of water, it would recede just beyond his reach. And whenever he would reach up to grab a piece of the lush fruit, the branch would raise just beyond his reach. His hell was to be constantly tempted by things that will always be just beyond his reach.

The word "tantalize" originates from the story of Tantalus. To be tantalized means that our expectations are stirred for something that can never be obtained. It is the hell of constantly being tempted by the allure of possessions or status that can never be ours.

The story of Tantalus is about a way of life that we can all find ourselves living—always grasping for something that we can never reach. This constant reaching is about our search for significance. Some of us try to acquire the accoutrements of success to show we have arrived. Others try to garner attention, appreciation, and accolades to show that we are somebody of value, proving our lives have significance. Sadly, all too often whatever we achieve, whatever praise we receive, is never quite enough.

Most of us think we have the self-awareness to wise up and realize that we need to redirect our focus. But because the allure of what we're pursuing is so great and always seems within reach, we keep stretching ourselves a little farther. Without realizing it, we are living like Tantalus. And living like Tantalus takes its toll.

> I think a twentysomething's biggest fear is insignificance.
> They want to have a role in something
> bigger than themselves.
>
> —Paul Angone

The pastor has been invited over to speak with Jill, a bright but struggling teenager. Her parents are concerned because she is becoming distant at home and her grades are slipping at school.

At first they thought it was typical teenage behavior, a phase that she was going through. But as time passes, she doesn't seem to be moving through a phase, just deeper into it. Not knowing where to turn, they call the pastor hoping that she can help.

As the conversation unfolds, Jill recalls her earlier, happy years, when the budget was tight but so was her family. Now her parents barely speak, and when they do, it is mostly nagging, bickering, and arguing. It becomes clear very quickly that for Jill the house feels more like a Frigidaire than a home, because of the coldness her mom and dad are showing toward one another.

Jill's parents have done well in their professions. They're esteemed, well paid, and have a home and cars that are like stripes on a military uniform showing their rank. But to achieve and maintain this status takes considerable time and energy. They don't have much time to spend with Jill, so they give her about anything she asks for. Jill makes clear that she isn't complaining about having the latest iPhone and a credit card covered by her parents, but the pastor senses that she's grieving the loss of her family, even though technically it remains "intact."

For years her parents have said that soon they will be able to slow down and spend more time with her, but it never seems to happen. There is always just a little more to do and a little more to achieve before they can redirect their priorities.

Before leaving, Jill points to the family portrait on the wall. It shows a family all snuggled together with smiling faces. While staring at the portrait, Jill says, "That's the family we wish we were, not who we really are."

It's not only a matter of strained relations in families with teenagers. The same parents who bicker and leave Jill sad likely have aging parents of their own, perhaps already widowed, likely living in a nursing home. Nearly ninety years old, Elizabeth sits primly in a rocking chair in her small room. She greets visitors warmly but a note of sorrow enters her words. "Once in a while my son phones, but he rarely visits," she says. "My granddaughter will call but she only talks about herself. They're so busy. I suppose I was when I was young." Elizabeth shares an odd and sad empathy with Jill, who is not the distracted granddaughter. There is little Elizabeth wants for care and comfort. But she wishes her family was more than related. Despite brief bursts of conversation that are distantly warm, something essential is missing.

Living like Tantalus is taking its toll on many of us. We feel the stress and emptiness, but we continue with the belief that if we reach just a little farther, we will finally get what we need to feel whole and complete. What we don't realize is that living like Tantalus is like walking on a treadmill: you're moving but you're going nowhere!

Seeking Significance in Generational Ways

We all seek significance. It is a fundamental human need. However, if we seek it in the wrong places, it will never be ours. It is here that faith and spirituality speak to this search by directing us toward that which truly leads to lives of significance. We know that by saying this, many will think that faith and religion can't possibly be the answer. We agree . . . sort of.

Culture is changing and younger generations are raising perspectives and questions to which the church has been unable to respond. Actually, it has responded, but often in ways that don't have any resonance. As we observed in *A Church Beyond Belief,* in the face of these challenges, congregations have tried to make beliefs more pronounced rather than the spiritual quest more profound. And they have yet to realize that faith is not static belief but a dynamic journey. There is a great need to reframe faith for a new generation—a generation that isn't quite like those who came before them.

In doing this we must recognize that though we all seek significance, we don't all see it or seek it in the same way. It isn't only that we have individual differences. We have generational differences.

This is a relatively new phenomenon. It used to be that "generations" referred to parents and grandparents. To say that we're from a different generation was to say that twenty-five-year-old Alison is different from her seventy-five-year-old grandmother because they are at a different phase in their life cycles. The assumption was that when Alison becomes seventy-five, she'll take on the values her grandmother had at that age.

Then we began to realize significant events could shape us. Going to war, experiencing a major economic recession, or witnessing the terror of 9/11 impacts us all. But the degree of impact it has on us depends upon our stage in life. Some say that 9/11 has had a particularly significant impact on Millennials, who were young children at the time. One study even cites that Millennials view 9/11 as the single greatest influence in shaping who they are.[5] Because of this, they have become more patriotic, more liberal, and more globally minded. Again, it is not that they are the only ones who were impacted. It is that it impacted them in more profound ways.

Finally, we came to understand that generations develop distinctive attitudes, beliefs, and approaches to life that will remain throughout their lives. The Greatest Generation, the Silent Generation, Baby Boomers, Baby Busters, Millennials, and Generation Z (becoming known as the Homeland Generation) each have a uniqueness about them so that there will always be a difference between generations, no matter where they in their life cycle. This means that Millennials and the Homelanders are right: they will never be quite like the rest of us. For older generations, this is difficult to accept. For younger generations, this is just the way things are.[6]

Generation Name[7]	Births Starting	Births Ending	Youngest Age Today	Oldest Age Today
The Greatest Generation	1910	1925	91	106
The Silent Generation	1923	1944	72	93
Baby Boomer Generation	1945	1964	52	71
Generation X Baby Busters	1961	1981	35	55
Generation Y The Millennials, Gen Next	1975	1995	21	41
Generation Z The Homeland Generation	1995	2015	1	21

Note: Dates are approximate and there is some overlap because there are no standard definitions for when a generation begins and ends.

From family life to politics, careers to relationships, this evolving sense of generations and claiming of a generational identity has forever shifted how we see the world. It is also having profound effects on how we see faith, spirituality, and the search for significance.

Faith Shifts

These changing generational dynamics are underpinned by shifts in our culture that are changing the way we view faith. These are not minor shifts. They are seismic. The two most impactful faith shifts are the release from religion and the phenomenon of choosing and rechoosing.

The Release from Religion

Millennials and the Homeland Generation don't realize this, but not long ago Christianity held a privileged place in our society. As a consequence, its values were imposed on everyone whether they were active in a church or not. Let us give one example that helps understand this.

When I (Michael) was growing up, every Sunday after church we drove to Grandmother's for dinner. On the drive, the neighborhoods we passed were always quiet. I can't recall seeing a single person doing yard work. This wasn't because they were all Christian and keeping the Sabbath. It was because the dominant religious culture dictated that one was to "rest" on Sundays.

Then things began to change. When I was about ten years old, for the first time I saw a person mowing their grass on Sunday while on the way to Grandma's. After pondering what I had just witnessed, I asked my father, "Is that man going to hell?" After a long pause he replied, "Only God knows, son. Only God knows." (A wise way to reframe a little boy's query.)

Boomers and Busters can all have stories that relate to this. The reality is that most generations before us experienced societal and kinship pressure that told us what we were to do and what we were to believe. Religious education was more about "Here's what you need to believe" rather than "What do you think about this?"

Today there has been a massive cultural shift away from what previous generations experienced. With the rise of religious pluralism and the diversity of religious expressions around us, there is no longer one dominant religious culture that informs what we can and can't do. We are free to believe or not believe. And yes, we can now mow our lawns whenever we damn well please! No longer do kinship pressure and a dominant religious culture dictate our beliefs and religious affiliations.

Younger generations have embraced the freedom to choose as the way it should be in all spheres of life. Currently, 71 percent of Millennials would prefer to quit their jobs and work for themselves because they want to make up their own rules. Employers beware: 61 percent of them plan on quitting in the next two years!

—Based on Tim Elmore's
"Six Millennial Statistics That Every Adult Should Know"

Religious diversity isn't just "out there." It is woven into the fabric of our intimate relationships. "Among Americans who have gotten married since 2010, nearly four-in-ten (39%) report that they are in religiously mixed marriages, compared with 19% among those who got married before 1960."[8]

We have truly become free agents in the religious market-place. And we are using our freedom to release ourselves from the dogma, doctrines, and religious observances of the past. We are able to determine for ourselves what it means to have faith and be spiritual. We can reject doctrines, select parts of them, or create our own religious mash-up from the "best of" the religions we encounter. Faith and religion are no longer hand-me-downs that we must accept. We are truly free to embrace that which has meaning for us.

The days are gone when Christianity determined the norms for all of us. We have moved in the opposite direction, where the act of being Christian and actively participating in a congregation are seen as countercultural acts. This is especially true in metro-urban contexts, where Sunday brunch is the new norm, not Sunday worship.

I'd never go out with a guy who lists himself
as Christian on his Tinder profile.

—Maureen, 25

While we celebrate the ability to choose our own faith commitments, or none at all, there has been a consequence to this personalization of religion. Because we are releasing ourselves from religion we no longer have a source or a community to which we look for wisdom and guidance. Instead, we have only ourselves. For many, we have come to the place where "we have the capacity to question everything but little ability to affirm anything."[9] This leads us to the second cultural shift impacting faith.

Choosing . . .

Once Joshua reached high school it dawned on him that he had choices. So despite a Protestant home and a Catholic school, he "eased away" from church as he recalled it. His body was there as little as possible, while his head and heart were gone. Asking "large questions" about life prompted his departure. Churches presented someone else's certainty. Joshua wanted to ask questions and explore options. No church spoke in those terms. He rejected the idea of being handed his identity; he wanted to find it for himself.

For increasing numbers of people life revolves around the exercise of choice. As luck would have it, there's no lack of options. In the city where one of us lives, the cable television system offers 1,952 channels for one of its multiple packages. Other viewing packages include more or fewer channels. One's choices also include having cable service "bundled" with Internet access, Wi-Fi, and telephone service. A home security system may also be added. Of course it could all be moot: a rival cable company offers other packages with alternative terms.

Connection to a "smart" television also brings "on demand" sources such as Netflix. One could also go wireless with one's own satellite dish and "direct" television; or one could revert to "rabbit ears" and receive only local broadcast programming. One could also be dismayed by all options, and the paucity of quality programs, and switch off one's television. Perhaps life would be better lived with a walk and a good book.

> We all create the person we become by our choices as we go through life. In a real sense, by the time we are adults, we are the sum total of the choices we have made.
>
> —Eleanor Roosevelt,
> *You Learn by Living*

Having choices has become a hallmark of freedom and individualism. The lack of choice, or restrictions on the ability to choose, feels like confinement, which we take personally. In all aspects of life, including work, relationships, home and neighborhood, hobbies, leisure, and of course religion, choice is a key requirement. By means of choice we set out on self-selected journeys to build the life we are inclined to seek, at least for now. Choice has become a presumed personal right. The exploration of options has become our pathway.

But "the fact that some choice is good doesn't necessarily mean that *more* choice is better," Barry Schwartz insists. In *The Paradox of Choice* he cites findings from a supermarket visit. In an ordinary market he found "85 different varieties and brands of crackers." There were "285 varieties of cookies," twenty-one of which had chocolate chips. Twenty varieties of "Goldfish" sat near thirteen "sports drinks," sixty-five "box drinks for kids," "85 other flavors and brands of juice, and 75 iced teas and adult drinks."[10] The point could be made on every store aisle, including cosmetics, health products, grooming and bath items, and even staples such as soup. Small wonder that such stores can provide sites for personal training. Patrolling such aisles becomes miles of walking.

The lure of options is compounded by the appeal of mixing and matching. Restaurants offering "fusion" food abound. Opportunities to match Asian and Latin American foods, to test "Mediterranean" or to have "comfort" dishes served in gourmet fashion draw hungry crowds. Varieties and mixtures served in entertaining styles have energized the food industry. Part of the allure is the chance to sample and to mix as one's inclinations direct. There also is the appeal of doing it for one's self, cooking spontaneously at home. Cookbooks and celebrity chefs and stores featuring exotic implements thrive, as do grocery stores.

Choice is not a passive quality; often it is cloaked in energetic initiative that extends beyond preparing meals. At a local outlet of a home goods chain, a man named Chet described his work as he adjusted a display. "Every class we offer is full," he commented. Chet then listed classes in basic plumbing, laying tile, finish carpentry, gardening, and roof repair. "It's a do-it-yourself generation," Chet concluded. It's also a generation that prizes choice.

Setting out to climb a mountain is no isolated instance. It offers a metaphor for life today, especially for young adults. The climb obviously involves feeling at one with nature and a friend. It presumes the opportunity to choose one's pursuits and one's associations, and the meaning of them, for oneself. It entails effort and presses one to acquire necessary skills. The result is a feeling of building and going and gaining one's real self, unhindered, unfettered, not prescribed. Choice is the basis for finding one's true self.

Faith is presumed to be the stuff of religion. It can loom like a mountain that one may choose to climb, or grocery aisles that one may choose to explore. One can go or not go as one chooses. One can select the occasion and the extent, going alone or with a friend. Along the aisles one can mix and match, varying selections, testing combinations. American religion now resembles a large market. Countless varieties of Christianity are evident: just the varieties of evangelical religion can be overwhelming. Roman Catholicism was never monolithic and now abounds in variation. A spectrum of Hispanic religion expands steadily, for example. Older distinctions such as liberal and conservative Protestants are now sliced into a variety of shapes.

... And Rechoosing

Once well over 90 percent Christian, the United States now is dipping to about 70 percent. The growth of non-Christian religions, notably Buddhism, Hinduism, and Islam, has been striking. More striking has been the growth of the Nones, persons with no religious affiliation. A steadily increasing number, approaching one-quarter of the population, many Nones are young adults of the Millennial (twenty-one to forty-one) generation. Roughly two-thirds believe in God or a higher power as they see it. Resolutely they reject atheism just as they avoid dogmatic religion. Instead, inwardly focused and outwardly driven, Nones want to find what is spiritually right for them today. Tomorrow they may choose differently.

Some see this as people becoming more fickle in their commitment. Claude Fischer, who analyzes social and cultural change, sees it differently. He says, "It is not that Americans are individualistic, they do believe in community, but it is a community that is voluntarily chosen and rechosen every day."[11]

People are certainly rechoosing religious affiliation. Studies show that nearly half of all Americans have changed their religious affiliation by changing churches, denominations, or faith traditions.[12] Some change because they're frustrated with church doctrine or dogma. Others change because they married someone from another tradition. Still others change because they wanted a different worship style. Interestingly, of those who were raised with no religious affiliation, half will belong to a community of faith as an adult.

This phenomenon has been labeled as a consumer mentality that has spawned competition between providers of religious goods and services. However, what people overlook in this reshuffling of religious affiliation, is that we are a highly mobile population. According to the U.S. Census, 35 percent of Americans have moved at least once in the last five years.[13] Therefore necessity as well as choice is driving the redistribution of religious affiliation.

A minister in a suburb of a city in the West experienced this impulse in her congregation. She was puzzled when a young couple who had been active suddenly vanished. They had been leaders, even committee chairs. Then they were gone. Had something happened? Had some offense been taken? The minister hastened to visit and the couple greeted her warmly. They felt no offense; in fact they loved the church. "But we decided we would become Buddhist next. Maybe we will be back. Maybe not." Apparently they sought intense involvement of brief duration. The phenomenon of rechoosing keeps choice alive more than lasting commitment.

The Wilderness of Choice

But choice carries various challenges. As Barry Schwartz describes, "We have too many choices, too many decisions, too little time to do what is really important." He sees frustrations arising from "missed opportunities" and from choices that fail to deliver the goods they promise. Moreover, we add, in a consumer society even moments of great satisfaction are ephemeral. The great meal or the enthralling movie or the fabulous trip come and go. Even a mountain climb, hopefully in good weather, will end. Ideally memories are created and life is savored. But if life is a series of mountaintop experiences, we are always in search of the next high.

Ideal circumstances do not always prevail. Storms arise. Technology balks. Meals fail to deliver. Promises of great experiences fall short. And so it goes. Far more than products, human relationships fray. Illness arises. Miscommunication arises. Fondly chosen dreams falter and crash. Few days of the week prove ideal. Much of our time is spent imagining while we plow through mundane details. Some of our time must be spent repairing and regrouping and trying to understand why such fine intentions went off the rails.

The sober truth is that life cannot simply be a matter of making choices and enjoying the results. So much of what we experience is the result of circumstances over which we had no choice: the life into which we were born is the prime instance. However fortunate or strained, we had no choice about our childhood. Similarly we inherited abilities that may not equip us for the dreams we cultivate. One of us may dream of repairing automobiles, but it will only be a dream. Even with ability, life's demands intervene, opening some doors while closing others. We do not have an infinite store of choices, nor unlimited ability, nor adequate time. Ideal conditions prove to be fleeting moments.

What shapes how we choose and what does the reality of choice have to do with faith? First, the emphasis on choice today shows the extent of our emphasis on individualism. We are determined to find our genuine selves, to live active and fulfilling lives, preferably as we would choose. Second, choice suggests our longing to take control of our lives in an uncertain world. Third, the choices we make reveal our trajectory, the direction we select in search of ourselves. Thus, our choices represent a pattern, a path. But does this path lead us to a worthy destination, or are we fumbling in the dark, amid random experiences, trying to find something lasting and good? Direction, purpose, values, and wholeness are attributes of faith, as we shall explain.

"It is our choices, Harry, that show what we truly are, far more than our abilities."

—J. K. Rowling
Harry Potter and the Chamber of Secrets

The pathway toward faith must pass through the wilderness of choice. We are assaulted by media images of enjoyment and satisfaction, wrapped around material things. Visions of a flourishing life drive us from one product to the next. We are drawn out of ourselves, hoping to reach somewhere worthwhile. But do we actually enhance our lives in this way? What endures when our choice of the moment fades? What holds life together; what is the glue that holds us together? Is there something more than avid but fragmented pursuits?

The essence of faith is making choices that lead us to a life of significance. Secular analysis of the proliferation of choices inevitably focuses on how to choose better, and not simply be stymied by too many options. Researcher and author Sheena Iyengar, for example, describes choice as an art. For her, the best choices point us toward patterns of meaning. Acts of interpretation are inherent; we are ever in search of grasping what our inclinations mean. Understanding the values we hold, but may not fully understand, can enlighten us on the choices we make.

But what sort of shape does life take, even when we understand our instincts? By what criteria do we consider our preferences and our actions? Until we open the category of faith, it is difficult to pin down what we really seek, how and what we trust, and who we really are. Faith points us toward clear answers to such questions, and toward an enduring and beneficial life. There is wholeness and purpose to be found beyond what we have imagined, or chosen.

Spiritual Anemia

Faith is a spiritual quest. And though interest in institutional religion is waning, there is a growing interest in things spiritual. However, the meaning of being "spiritual" has changed, making it hard to define. A recent study found ninety-two definitions for spirituality, and still growing. This has left us with vague notions of what spirituality is, what one does to become spiritual, and how we develop our spirituality.

Amidst this shift, Lucy Bregman has observed that there is a major difference between our present day understanding of spirituality and how it has been understood in the past. Spirituality has been rooted in the idea that it was "two-poled, in other words: it has an 'outward' or objective pole and an 'inward' or subjective pole."[14] Today it has become one-poled, only focusing upon the inward aspect of being spiritual. Spirituality has come to mean a "natural potential in all of us" to be spiritual. It is an innate aspect of who we are. Bregman notes, "That is why in the more recent literature, it is rare to find someone ask directly, 'How do I become spiritual?' The answer is: you do not need to become; you already are." This has left people with vague notions of what one can do with the spirituality that resides within us.

What is missing is the outward pole, which is "an intentional pursuit of something beyond the self." Our observation is that spirituality without an outward pole easily becomes self-centered and self-serving. This is why in the midst of a growing emphasis on spirituality, it has lacked the vitality needed to move people toward a life of significance.

Looking beyond Oneself

In looking for significance we must look beyond ourselves. It's that simple. And if our spirituality does not point us in this direction, we will experience it as anemic and we will be unable to find the spiritual, psychological, and emotional health and wholeness we seek.

Martin Seligman, a pioneer in positive psychology, says that in order for us to flourish we also must serve something larger than we are.[15] Jonathan Haidt, a prominent social psychologist, notes that "religious people are happier, on average, than nonreligious people. This effect arises from the social ties that come with participation in a religious community, as well as from feeling connected to something beyond the self."[16]

Mircea Eliade, an influential historian of religions, observed that throughout history humanity has displayed a need for the sacred, something larger than ourselves. He observed that "Regardless of their differences, all religions have places (temples, shrines, holy trees), times (holy days, sunrise, solstices), and activities (prayer, special dancing) that allow for contact or communication with something otherworldly and pure."[17] Eliade believed that for the first time in history, Western culture has stripped the sacred, that something more, from our lives so that all we have left is the profane. Given this, it explains why a spirituality that is self-centered leaves so many of us feeling that life is mundane.

And then we come to Jesus, who when pressed about which commandment is greatest, he replied: "'You shall love the Lord your God with all your heart, and with all your soul, and with all your mind.' This is the greatest and first commandment. And a second is like it: 'You shall love your neighbor as yourself.' On these two commandments hang all the law and the prophets" (Matt. 22:37–40).

There are two things that are important about Jesus's response. First, it emphasizes the choices we make. To refer to one's "heart" is to focus on "the center of a person's willing, *choosing,* doing."[18] Second, it is outward-focused, toward God and others. It is not on ourselves.

The ancient wisdom of Jesus that has been passed on to us has now been researched by sociologists, psychologists, and historians, and as we have seen, they come to the same conclusion. If you want significance, if you want true happiness, if you want to find meaning, then choose to live for something larger than yourselves. When we squander our choices on things that are insignificant, we live insignificant lives. When we choose things that have ultimate significance, then we live lives of significance. As we move to the coming chapters, we discover that the Christian faith guides us toward the things that matter most.

A Question to Consider How much should our faith tradition guide and inform our choices, and how much should it tell us what those choices should be?

A Thing You Can Do Talk with others and draw upon your faith tradition to help you articulate what has ultimate significance in your life. Knowing this is what directs your decisions toward that which matters most.

CHAPTER 2

Awakening to Wonder

Enchanted Worlds

Every few weeks Dave posts pictures from his latest hike on Facebook. Often with friends, sometimes alone, he regularly turns to the outdoors, especially national parks, where he finds himself amid spectacular beauty. His photos can offer striking panoramas of hills and valleys, lakes and fields. He can also zero in on particular plants, especially in bloom, and animals, especially birds. Always energized by being in nature, Dave finds the experience brings more than physical conditioning. He seeks, and regularly feels, a connection to something genuine, something larger than himself. A turn in the path offers an unexpected new vista. Even if he has been there before, he still finds something new, some new perspective. Dave likes seeing things he has never seen, or glimpsing them from new angles, with shade and clouds unlike a previous visit. Above all he returns feeling connected beyond himself. Dubious about religion, and especially religious institutions, he embraces spirituality, yet hesitates to define it too narrowly. Perhaps without knowing it, Dave stands on the threshold of faith.

Pam also ventures into nature, but not as adventurously as hiking trails in remote areas. A skilled photographer, she is more apt to visit a local park or nearby beach, usually with several lenses and filters for her camera. She has acute vision, and particular skill at quickly framing an appealing scene. The brief, feeding pause of a hummingbird will not escape her. Strolling robins and even boastful crows catch her fancy. Nature's interactions bring endless fascination. Her close-up studies circulate quickly on social media. The pictures often are striking. Pam likes going out on her own, how and when the mood strikes her. She admits that it strikes often.

Now that she is retired, Linda stays closer to home, but with no less appreciation and equally elaborate results. In warm weather her garden overflows with luscious vegetables and fruit. Friends encourage her to open a stand on a nearby corner but she shrugs and laughs. Her tomatoes and squash, cucumbers and berries, wind up in elaborate recipes for various guests, always drawing rave reviews. An invitation to her home is coveted. Her sense of nature includes sampling as well as admiring. She likes to experiment in the kitchen with different combinations, always using freshly grown foods and matching them with fine wines. In the process she convenes people and fosters warm conversations. The feeling of connection is shared and rich. Nature's bounty has solidified friendships.

The human fascination with nature is timeless. On June 3, 1805, the explorer Meriwether Lewis recorded the latest view of nature he and his party had discovered. Referring to his colleague, William Clark, Lewis noted:

> Capt. C & myself strolled out to the top of the
> heights in the fork of these rivers from whence
> we had an extensive and most inchanting (sic)
> view; the country in every direction around us

was one vast plain in which innumerable herds of Buffalow (sic) were seen attended by their shepherds the wolves.[19]

Why do so many people seek occasions to be in contact with nature? For some of us being outdoors involves hunting and fishing, or sailing, or rowing, or hiking, or skiing. Some love to camp and a few even dare to explore caves, often in remote locations. For others of us the outdoors means cultivating and growing, usually right on our own property. Still others seek to find precious moments of interaction that they might capture as still and video photography. For them nature is less to be mastered than to be admired. Nature's appeal is practically universal, and to say some product or experience is "natural" is to attest to its authenticity and its quality.

Something Spiritual

Nature represents more than a respite from daily routines and more even than discovery and exploration. We are more apt to speak of "spirituality" in relation to nature than in any other setting. Even people who resist religion find themselves drawn to speak of spirituality when the natural world is invoked, including the natural order beyond our own planet. The astrophysicist Neil deGrasse Tyson has observed that "when I say spiritual, I'm referring to a feeling you would have that connects you to the universe in a way that it may defy simple vocabulary."[20]

There are places and moments in which one is so completely alone that one sees the world entire.

—Attributed to Jules Renard

Tyson's point is crucial for us. "Spirituality" is often thought to be confined to our inner selves, our thoughts and feelings, our clear intentions, and our struggles for clarity and purpose. But Tyson, like people who hike, photograph, and garden, locates spirituality on a different plane. Spirituality is not ourselves alone. As we explored in chapter 1, spirituality comes alive when it points us beyond ourselves and toward vital connections. The liveliness of such connections, and our need for them, are never more apparent than in nature, even in a backyard or nearby park.

No wonder that particular places, especially at certain times of the year, become laden with memories and meanings. A particular stretch of coast or turn in a beach, a certain hill or mountain, a valley, a bend in a river, a point in a park, all can become, well, sacred. They have the quality of the "numinous," meaning they bring significance to aspects of our lives and awaken a sense of connecting to something basic, deeper, more authentic, truly whole. In such places, at such moments, perhaps with someone significant in our lives, we have found lasting insight and purpose. The place becomes laden with that meaning. To return there is to return to a notable time in life. We recapture the feeling, and we feel the wonder of the moment again. We recover clarity and purpose and worth in such places.

Nature is one of life's key bridges to the spiritual. Particular places and moments open up broad meaning. So we seek to return, even to create regular participation in such places. We find, over and over, that to truly be, we must be somewhere. For reasons we find difficult to put into words, a certain scene captures us in ways that other scenes cannot. Somehow we feel at home, feel both free and joined, find ourselves and feel ourselves found. John has a difficult time describing why saltwater fishing captivates him, but it does. Something about the waves and the water, and a limitless horizon enthrall him. The day is better if he catches fish, but that is never the whole point. The act of being on the water touches him. On land he is always eager to return to the waves. Even bad weather enlivens him and energizes the descriptions his family expects.

Not every fishing trip ends with safe returns and happy accounts. In *The Perfect Storm*, author Sebastian Junger recounts the story of the *Andrea Gail*, a New England fishing vessel that vanished in 1991 when caught in a storm of freak intensity. The story gained wide notice as a movie as well as a book. It drove home the variety of human encounters with nature. Serenity can turn dramatically to violence and danger. Nature is the setting for powerful aspects of the human spiritual journey, in part because both good and evil are dramatized there. When we venture outdoors, we presume to know what we will find, and that is part of the joy as well as the risk. We always find that surprising realities await.[21]

In 1854 the noted writer Henry David Thoreau published his memoir of two years spent living alone near Walden Pond in Massachusetts. It was nearly ten years after he first went there, but the reflections were vivid and powerful. His time in nature had solidified deep convictions.

> I went to the woods because I wished to live deliberately, to front only the essential facts of life, and see if I could not learn what it had to teach, and not when I came to die, discover that I had not lived. I did not wish to live what was not life, living is so dear; nor did I wish to practice resignation, unless it was quite necessary.[22]

The experience linked Thoreau to various religious and spiritual traditions. He noted that he had read Hindu scriptures, for instance. But the purpose was not simply to connect to religious tradition, though that may have been something of a by-product. Rather he reported a sense of awakening, of elevating his life, as all people could elevate theirs, "by conscious endeavor. It is something to be able to paint a particular picture, or to carve a statue . . . . but it is far more glorious to carve and paint the very atmosphere and medium through which we look, which morally we can do." Thoreau had discovered that he could recast his own life. To do so, he had to turn outward as well as inward. When he did, he saw the world and himself anew.

> Earth's crammed with heaven,
> And every common bush, afire with God.
>
> —Elizabeth Barrett Browning,
> "Aurora Leigh"

Like many others then and now, Thoreau experienced a sense that nature is sacred, and that being human means we share in it. That is, nature is to be venerated because there we find goodness and purpose from beyond ourselves. There is discovery of a greater reality, a "higher power," offering us a feeling of completion. The feeling awakens us because we begin to see what we have never glimpsed, like explorers in uncharted land. In a spiritual sense, the land has been there all along, like mountain trails or paths in public parks we have never followed. The land awaits our visit. In that sense we discover it.

Like such byways, our own lives await eye-opening discovery. This is nature's symbolic appeal. It represents our lives, complex landscapes never genuinely plumbed, much less ever truly appreciated. How we treat nature reflects how we treat ourselves and the people to whom we are linked. Our preoccupations can distract us from looking deeply. Our fears may convince us that what we would see may disappoint or even harm us. But there is no spirituality, and no whole self, without daring to look deeply. The benefit outweighs the cost. There is no greater benefit than awakening and seeing, perhaps for the first time.

Visions of Faith

Because it is tangible and vivid, nature readily triggers feelings of connection beyond ourselves. Limitless vistas, changing scenes, and the bounty of life in its variations alert us to realities we had not imagined. The celebrated photographer Ansel Adams observed that some who step into nature "impose the domination of their own thought and spirit. Others come before reality more tenderly and a photograph to them is an instrument of love and revelation."[23]

The essence of faith is making choices that lead to a life of significance. We must choose to be in nature, exposing ourselves to its whims. Nevertheless our own agendas and assumptions easily dominate our awareness of what we find. The choice to be alert and open produces a strikingly different outcome. We can realize that we are seeing realities we have overlooked, even if we had reached the same spot on a prior visit. We can also begin to see possibility and promise in nature that can awaken us to a life we have not yet lived. We see what has been there all along. We awaken to it and feel at home in it. There is something profound before us and we have awakened to it.

If the natural world readily evokes spirituality, a key aspect is sight or, more lyrically, vision. In this respect spirituality is the beginning of the pathway toward faith, and spirituality is evoked powerfully in nature. There we begin to see, and not abstractly. We feel tangibly drawn into what we glimpse. Asked what they feel

amid their explorations, Dave and Pam, Linda and John use similar words. Wonder. Beauty. Awe. Serenity. Purpose. Connection.
Their words echo Thoreau, though their stays in nature are never
so extended.

Nature becomes an analogy for each of them. It is more than
escape. The vision they have acquired outdoors translates into
their lives indoors. They "see" more deeply into work as well as
recreation. Mundane tasks become pieces of a larger whole. There
is greater possibility in life for them; they are able to take creative,
beneficial control of their lives. They "see" more deeply also into
family and friends, often with as much gratitude as insight. They
are more likely to become specific about what really matters in
life, and they are more inclined to care actively about the struggles of other people. What were once brief glimpses of life, as if
looking from beyond it amid one's preoccupations, has become
more of a vision and a connection. They feel a part of what they
experience. That feeling represents an awakening. They begin to
see; they have vision.

For centuries people have experienced visions, often in nature,
and have understood them as pathways to sacred reality. In 1437,
a philosopher and Catholic cleric named Nicholas of Cusa experienced something of a vision while onboard a ship sailing across
the Mediterranean. Noting that at the horizon, sea and sky met,
he realized that sacred reality, or God, must be both transcendent
or beyond nature, and immersed in it. In other words, what we
experience in nature points beyond, to greater reality, yet grounds
our lives in vital connections to the natural order.

Nicholas of Cusa would have another vision that was striking
for his age. Perhaps from his shipboard experience, he concluded
that earth and all creation are not static. The natural world, and
our planet itself, are in motion, constant motion. To find the
sacred, or God, we must also be in motion. Refusing to stand
still, we must see life as activity, and we must become part of that

dynamism. Then we open ourselves to sacred reality. Without saying it in quite this way, Nicholas posed the idea that faith is rooted in vital connection to the world around us.[24]

If there is a crisis of faith today, and this would not be the first such time in human history, it is a crisis of connection. Countless people today only feel connected—to nature, to other people, and to institutions—in fragile ways, if at all. The idea of discovering that each of us is linked to deeper reality, in fact that we can see through nature to that reality, gives us pause. Such a discovery and the reality to which it points seem dubious.

> The world is so empty if one thinks only of mountains, rivers & cities; but to know someone who thinks and feels with us, and who, though distant, is close to us in spirit, this makes the earth for us an inhabited garden.
>
> —Attributed to Johann Wolfgang von Goethe

If there are connections to be built, many people assume, they can only be tangible, even empirical. Deeper reality, it is widely presumed, is not waiting to be discovered, it can only be built by dogged human effort. Accordingly, if there is faith to be found, we must find it within ourselves, many people affirm. At stake is our personal freedom, our right to design life as we choose, or so it is widely and profoundly felt. Spirituality, to the extent that we emphasize its importance for our lives, is welcome. Religion presumably would tell us what to think and what to do. Many people reject all religions because they appear to emphasize order and control.

But like the accounts of Nicholas of Cusa, visions of various sorts clutter human history, and make the boundary between religion and spirituality a fuzzy one. It is not easy to say that human experience of greater reality, however it is posed, is either purely spiritual or religious. Visions sit at an important intersection. They push one toward patterns of meaning that prompt particular actions and even entire ways of life. One's understanding and relation to the world and to other people deepen. One seeks to ground one's experience and often one finds guidance in religious tradition as well as spiritual precedent.

The reality is that religion does not dictate or confine: it frames and empowers an experience by explaining it in terms of precedent. The vision gives rise to activity, uniting people who have shared the experience. In that sense, a vision, or what people report they have seen, especially in relation to nature, is inherently true. It is confirmed by the fact that people claim it and act on the basis of it.

Of course, visions, and human behavior resulting from them, have varied dramatically. In 1931, on a hillside in the Basque area of northern Spain, children reported that they had seen a vision of the Virgin Mary. The hill, near the town of Ezquioga, quickly became a pilgrimage site. A social movement arose, defying the opposition of religious as well as political authorities. More than one million people visited the site before such visits were proscribed. The "truth" of the vision was not limited to whether or not the Virgin Mary literally appeared there. The "truth" lay in the power of the place and the experience to stir human hearts, to link people in common cause, and to prompt concerted action. The truth of the experience was such that political and religious institutions perceived a threat and acted to squelch it.[25]

The outbreak of religious visions on a Basque hilltop reveals much about spirituality and religion, as well as visions in nature. The Spanish episode demonstrates that such visions have freed people to see life as whole, to feel themselves affirmed, and to see themselves in vital connection beyond their individual selves.

Such visions readily challenge existing categories of religious belief and practice as posed by institutions. We often find that institutional presumption wilts in the face of such spiritual immediacy and connection. The lesson should not be lost on us: faith is based in vital connection beyond ourselves.

Moments of Awakening

How do such connections arise? How do they relate to the sorts of visions we depict? We have spoken broadly of "awakening," a term that refers to a new and life-changing awareness which could not be planned or anticipated. Such an awakening could arise from one's first glimpse of a place one has never been, as Lewis and Clark repeatedly experienced on their historic expedition. But awakenings as we understand them also represent seeing familiar places and situations and people in entirely new ways. The place one has seen before, and the people in it, reveal new dimensions of reality that capture one's attention differently, for the first time.

What becomes paramount in an awakening is that the newly seen reality is not viewed casually or from a distance. What one glimpses is immediate, compelling, personal. There is a powerful sense of being drawn into the vision, of participating in it. Such a turn in one's life could not have been anticipated. With a vision that compels participation, an empowering sense of clarity unfolds. Vision means understanding, and understanding of this sort reshapes how one sees the rest of life, including oneself. There can even be a powerful, moral compulsion: the vision has such power that one feels one's life remade by it. There can also be an urgent feeling of responsibility to live according to what one has seen and felt. "Vision" becomes a broad idea, uniting sights, feelings, convictions, memories, priorities, norms, and intentions.

> Once the soul awakens, the search begins and you can never go back. From then on, you are inflamed with a special longing that will never again let you linger in the lowlands of complacency and partial fulfillment.
>
> —John O'Donohue,
> *Anam Cara: A Book of Celtic Wisdom*

We speak of awakenings, but such moments sound suspiciously like what has been called "conversion." Reference to conversion brings to the surface images of the least appealing aspects of religion. Conversion suggests a decisive change from a past that one rejects as one embraces a set of religious teachings and practices. Buttressed by images of religious extremism and sectarianism, conversion seems to imply compulsion, the rejection of uncertainty, submission to authoritarian influences, and hostility toward all outside one's like-minded group.

Conversion also suggests hysteria and actions taken that defy reason and common sense, even ordinary morality. A person who has been converted seems to have been influenced, even manipulated, perhaps against one's will. In the popular mind, conversion is the surrender, and maybe the abuse, of one's self. It is likely to occur as a group phenomenon where peer pressure is difficult to resist. In the wake of conversion there appears to be little room for questioning or further exploration. The convert seemingly must submit like a recruit in military boot camp. There is no room for doubt or reconsideration. The answers to life's questions have been found and need only be held firmly.[26]

The proliferation of religious cults and fundamentalist groups appears to confirm this popular image of conversion. The history of religious revivals also appears to justify viewing conversion as akin to hysteria fostered by personal vulnerability and used by unscrupulous authority figures. There is enough evidence, historically and in the present, that conversion is shrouded in unappealing imagery.

In fact, genuine instances of conversion throughout religious history closely resemble what we have called "awakening." Such experiences have indeed been compelled or used for unsavory purposes in some circumstances. But that is hardly the norm. More often conversion has represented the opening of a new pathway in life where none had been perceived; one's life heads in an unforeseen direction by previously unknown means. Thus, late in the fourth century, a young man sitting in a garden heard a child's voice where no child could be seen. As a result, this young man, named Augustine, picked up a nearby Christian Bible. Randomly he turned to Romans 13, verses 13–14. There he read words encouraging him to set aside the wanton life he had led and to live in a righteous way.

The young man became Christian and after this moment in a garden, in 386 CE, he would become one of Christianity's greatest leaders. To later generations he would be known as St. Augustine. In that light it has been tempting to view his conversion and subsequent life as a matter of spiritual certainty and religious obedience. From a distance his moment in the garden seemingly erased all doubt and any room for questions and revisions. Augustine himself seems to confirm this idea in his autobiography, *The Confessions*. The certainty and zeal of the convert shine through his words and confirm our suspicions.[27]

Over the centuries since his life, Augustine has been depicted as a foremost early Christian leader and thinker. He has been described, and could readily be understood, as polemical and inflexible, even an example of intolerance. Certainly he faced an array of religious and political opponents, against whom he maintained strong theological opinions. But a careful reading of his life adds another dimension. Like any person of faith, his life was a journey along which circumstances forced him to make choices and to act on them. Rarely could Augustine simply proclaim ideals and enforce them directly. Complex situations forced him to respond in ways that were tested. At times his ability to live faithfully was unclear, even strained. His faith did not waver; but it was shaped and reshaped in life's maelstrom.

> Men go abroad to wonder
> at the heights of mountains,
> at the huge waves of the sea,
> at the long courses of the rivers,
> at the vast compass of the ocean,
> at the circular motions of the stars, and
> they pass by themselves without wondering.
>
> —Saint Augustine

Centuries later, another man, also a budding author, awakened to the life of faith, though hardly in a garden in the ancient world. An American, Thomas Stearns Eliot lived in England because of his work. There he found more of a home than he expected. In 1927, Eliot found the Christian faith and the Church of England. Already known as T. S. Eliot, he outlined this awakening to faith in "Ash Wednesday," a characteristically allusory and intricate poem, published in 1930. There Eliot traced his movement beyond exile from himself and from the world. The right time and the right life are not where we imagine, he had realized. Instead we must surrender precious illusions and move toward what we begin to see within and around us.

In "Ash Wednesday," Eliot describes a fountain that springs up and a bird that begins to sing. There is a dawning sense of call to redeem time, to shed falsehood, to care generally. There is a sense of place for us, if we sit still to discover it. Separation can be overcome, he urges, using the imagery of a river's flow and of the sea's grandeur. Eliot writes as if committing a prayer to paper. Yet there is celebration, even exuberance. Life may be "this brief transit where the dreams cross/The dreamcrossed twilight between birth and dying." But in our brief time there is the possibility of choosing and awakening to lasting significance. Eliot makes the prospect of faith vivid and tangible.[28]

The experience of awakening to faith can evoke a high degree of certainty. It is natural to conclude that we have truly grasped what is certain, its truth and import appear evident. But regardless of the degree of certainty about newly found faith, once we have experienced such an awakening we must move ahead into uncertain and often uncontrollable life circumstances. Even firm confidence that one has found truth does not shield one from future challenges or uncertainties. Even with the most vigorous conviction, one must face life's contingencies. The experience of awakening—or conversion, for essentially they are the same—does not answer all questions or resolve all uncertainties. But one likely feels drawn to follow where this new path leads. What one finds along the way remains to be seen. Further vision awaits.

What Does It Mean?

Wonder is the basis of faith. We are especially struck by wonder in the midst of nature. There words such as "sacred" seem especially appropriate. The natural world awakens us to what is authentic, real. At the same time the natural world points beyond itself and invites us to an experience of discovery. In part, nature brings wonder to many of life's moments, infusing the mundane with points of meaning. In part the wonder of nature connects us to wider worlds, including people and places. We acquire feelings of connection to larger reality that transcends yet permeates us. Often that larger reality is called "God."

David Brooks has observed that faith is not "a simple holding of belief, or a confidence in things unseen; in real life, faith is unpredictable and ever-changing." Faith dawns in wonder that senses reality beneath life's surface. The "business of faith," as Brooks names it, is "being attentive every day." This entails using "sensations of holiness to inspire concrete habits, moral practices and practical ways of living well." Brooks means that faith is not a steady state, a rock to which we cling for security. Nor is faith a matter of right or wrong, of who is worthy and who fails the test. Quite the opposite, faith "is change. It is restless, growing." Within daily life there is ever-fresh possibility, benefit to be discovered and then to be shared. Being a genuine part of the wonder around us is a constant opportunity and challenge.[29]

But what do such moments of wonder mean? More pointedly, does our intrigue with wonder represent undue focus on ourselves? The question must be pressed. There have long been assertions that narcissism is prominent, perhaps even the defining feature of American life. By some accounts there is now an epidemic of narcissism, especially among young adults. The obvious signs are grandiosity, entitlement, and self-centeredness. At a deep level, the narcissistic personality is prone to seek, or assume, celebrity status and imagined, impending success. In a nutshell, narcissism is an inflated view of the self, excluding the perceptions and sensitivities of other people and their circumstances. One's self and one's gratification dominate.

There may be widespread evidence of narcissism and many of us may be susceptible to it. But two factors must be considered. First, narcissism, albeit prominent, can sound like a luxury to a different group of people. Countless people live with pain and hurt. Untold numbers carry not over-inflated views of themselves, but under-inflated views. Narcissism is countered by people who wrestle with depression, withdrawal, and defeatism. They may also be locked within themselves. But they act out of very different perceptions. Survival, not the next conquest, defines their challenge. Second, faith does not entail going within ourselves to ratify our lives as they are. Faith opens up both new perceptions of the world, and encouragement to connect outside ourselves in life-giving ways. Our individual selves have incredible, inherent worth. But we are incomplete without the ongoing experience of connection to others in true mutuality. Such connection is forged by awakening to transcendence, the dawn of conviction that we find wholeness when we are led by a power beyond our grasp, to a life we had not thought possible. By faith we perceive that this power calling us forth is the source and dynamism of all creation.

> It's what we trust in but don't yet see that keeps us going.
>
> —2 Corinthians 5:7,
> THE MESSAGE

But isn't this just a way of identifying a psychological mechanism within us, and not a defining power without? Aren't we depicting a dynamic more insidious than narcissism? For centuries there have been claims that religion is psychological projection devised for individual assurance, perhaps drawn from primitive views of nature and otherwise natural forces. Some avowed atheists have concluded that religion has been a tool for subjugation, a justification of unjust social relations, benefitting a few at the expense of the many. In that sense religion could be depicted as social narcissism. Undue glorification of societies and those who rule them forms an unfortunate, historic pattern.

Might faith, based in wonder and connection outside ourselves, be a matter of projection, however elaborate? Have our biological selves devised such moments of experience and the categories we use to explain them? Such questions are not so easily or conclusively addressed. They force us to move from observing the world, and hesitating to commit ourselves, to reaching a decision, a commitment about who we are and what we actually believe. Faith is ultimately an unavoidable question. By asking whether it is a matter of projection, we realize that we must answer the question: is faith in our imaginations just a matter of hallucination?

The noted neurologist and author Oliver Sacks has addressed this question substantively. Amassing medical case studies, often of rare and bizarre instances, Sacks presses the issue. He also cites historical evidence. For centuries people have had "apparitions" or sightings that mimic reality but are not there as they imagine them to be. Perceptions born of mental process are used to frame the external world. Now, with advances in neuroscience and in the treatment of obviously aberrant perceptions, the subject of mental process and its reference points has opened up. Interestingly, fresh insights have not simply consigned hallucinations and human visions generally to the realm of the imagination. Neither true perceptions of the world, nor dreams and fantasies of it, hallucinations form "a unique and special category of consciousness and mental life." They can be taken neither literally nor as madness.[30]

The coincidence of religious convictions with mental and physical experiences is apparent. Sacks cites the Russian writer Fyodor Dostoevsky, who had seizures that produced ecstatic and transcendent feelings. In his writing Dostoevsky depicted characters who found serenity and hope amid intense moments of internal light. Such times became revelations of direct truth because they were the presence of God, he felt. Sacks doesn't endorse such a view but he is struck by it. There may be a biological basis of religious experience. But that begs the question of "the value, the meaning, the 'function' of such emotions, or of the narratives and beliefs we may construct on their basis." In other words, biology alone does not answer the question of faith. Biology may be the mechanism but it is not the meaning. The question of faith remains before us, a crossroads of whether and how to believe in our minds and in our lives.

But does it all have a valid reference, or is it a matter of projection? Is there God or not? At the end of *Hallucinations*, Sacks offers a poignant thought:

> Thus the primal, animal sense of "the other," which may have evolved for the detection of threat, can take on a lofty, even transcendent function in human beings. As a biological basis for religious passion and conviction, where the "other," the "presence," becomes the person of God.[31]

Faith is grounded less in belief than in relatedness to the "other," that is, to the world and people outside ourselves. In times of genuine wonder, we can awaken to the reality around us, and seek connection to it, just as we can discover nature and our relation to it. We can feel a larger sense of reality that is beyond yet within us. We can also feel compelled to continue to awaken, to follow this reality and even to have our lives transformed in light of it. The truth of the reality beyond us surfaces in the life that we feel drawn to build because of it.

"What if these things are true?" A man named John Newton asked himself this question repeatedly nearly three hundred years ago. He was English and went to sea as a young man. There he quickly developed nautical skills and would rise to become a ship's captain. There he also continued a struggle between a search for faith and a morally questionable life. Then, when Newton was still a young man of twenty-three, in 1748, his ship was caught in a violent storm and was disabled. Newton's survival and that of his shipmates was in doubt. Somehow they stayed afloat; though some of the crew was lost, Newton survived. His life spared against all odds became an answer to the question that had haunted Newton. "These things," namely the reality of faith in the ultimate power called God, were true.

> I am not what I ought to be, I am not what I want to be,
> I am not what I hope to be in another world;
> but still I am not what I once used to be,
> and by the grace of God I am what I am.
>
> —John Newton

He swore off his dissolute lifestyle. Eventually he gave up the sea and became a priest of the Church of England. Soon he became known for hymns he authored, some of which reflected the faith he had found, and the awakening that prompted it. Among the many hymns for which Newton became known and that remain current, one has been especially notable:

> Amazing grace! (how sweet the sound)
>   That saved a wretch like me!
> I once was lost, but now am found,
>   Was blind, but now I see.

The power of Newton's transformation, and the vision it prompted, are apparent. They remain compelling. The extent of Newton's legacy is attested by generations of people seeking faith who have resonated with his struggle, his encounter with the power of nature, and the lasting faith that resulted. Looking back, it seems appropriate to speak of Newton's conversion as decisive, complete, and confident. There appears to be little room for doubt that faith awakened whole and decisively remade his life.[32]

In fact, after the initial, inner struggle, and even after the storm that he cited as the turning point, Newton's passage to faith was incomplete. Conversion in the history of religious life is never total or accomplished at once. Even if faith blossoms and never fades, it is made whole in subsequent stages. Together these later steps have been known as sanctification, or growth in holiness. Newfound assurance will be tested in the maelstrom of life's challenges. What it means to live as a person of faith will be sorted out in practical terms. One's relatedness to the world changes. One's priorities shift as old patterns of behavior give way to new ones. A new person is being born.

Sanctification is the process of living as a genuinely faithful person. Faith remains incomplete if held merely as a matter of personal feeling or a list of personal beliefs. It is incomplete if only one moment is cherished and not subsequent stages. Faith is proven by how the awakened person revises relations to other people and to the wider world. The reality that faith is more than feeling is verified. Sanctification entails morality or standards of behavior, but it cannot turn legalistic or prohibitive; sanctification concerns the life to be embraced, not simply the life to be renounced. Faith concerns who we become, not who we cease to be.

For John Newton this meant an eventual rejection of slavery and the slave trade, in which he had participated as a sea captain. Later in life he joined the emerging abolition movement. He did not live to see England abolish slavery, which occurred by an act of Parliament in 1833. But he awakened to the moral urgency of abolition and in that regard he continued the journey of faith. Indeed, faith must ever be a journey, its ramifications never fully grasped, its effect on our lives always awaiting further discovery. At times such journeys are wanderings. But as we awaken they become pilgrimages, and we become pilgrims.

A Question to Consider What have been your moments of "awakening to wonder," and how have they created a new and life-changing awareness within you?

A Thing You Can Do Consider the one or two choices you can make today that will lead to a life of greater significance.

CHAPTER 3

Becoming a Pilgrim

Finding a Thin Place

What is it like to see something for the first time? The question obviously refers to places we have never been but for some reason find ourselves. After Allison, a gifted writer, visited New Mexico for the first time, also her first visit to the American West, she recorded vivid images of the experience.

> I had never been to the West, had never seen the desert, had never seen anything like what I was seeing—the sage and juniper, the pinyon and cottonwood trees . . . . Everything was almost unbearably beautiful. I kept thinking that— unbearably beautiful . . . .
>
> One evening . . . I was sitting outside in the darkness and the stars were like a blanket I was underneath—so thick, so plentiful, with lightning around the edges of the sky that I felt I

was *inside* the Milky Way. From where I sat I
could hear my new friend Elmer playing the
Native American double flute. And I thought
this, right now, this is what is real.[33]

It was more than the vegetation or the landscape, as compelling as they proved to be. There for a weeklong retreat, Allison
was already poised to look beneath life's surface. Even so, what
she discovered proved arresting, as if a door to a new world had
opened. It was a door to God. "From what I understand, at least,
when we are experiencing God . . . there are no barriers, no walls,
no ego, no *self* getting in the way, and instead there is only the
spirit, the essence, the right now-ness of beauty, the singular relationship with God."

That is, she continued, this remote setting in New Mexico is
a "thin place, a place where the space between heaven and earth
collapses, where the walls weaken and another dimension seems
nearer than usual." There, "God feels closest, where I feel sometimes terrifyingly alive, when what is inside of me and what is outside of me feel close to being reconciled." When she is not there,
"it is the place . . . for which I am longing."

There are many journeys, many discoveries, many new
places, many reasons for going where we go. And there are many
places that promise to be "thin," that is, to draw us toward what
is real. The pursuit is deeply personal and not necessarily religious. In *Up in the Air*, his novel that was made into a movie,
Walter Kirn describes the travels of Ryan Bingham. At one level,
Bingham is a hard-charging business consultant. He works for a
firm that directs corporate restructurings for various companies.
This means he travels across the country telling people they are
losing their jobs. As George Clooney portrays him in the film,
Bingham acts implacably. He has no moral or emotional concern
for the people he faces. He announces their demotion in a dry

voice and reviews severance packages mechanically. He hardly sees what Allison saw in the desert.

Bingham's passion lies elsewhere, far from concern for human despair. He is obsessed with one avid pursuit to which his job is incidental. Bingham wants to earn one million frequent flyer miles, along with assorted points in hotel rewards programs. Always in transit from one restructuring to the next, Ryan Bingham encounters other road warriors and occasionally his encounters turn sexual. But, just as he discounts the importance of the people he fires, Bingham treats such trysts as incidental to his grand scheme. He is driven to reach a lofty frequent flyer mile goal and thinks of little else. When one promising relationship falters he quickly returns to his private pursuit.[34]

The story is fiction, a good read and an interesting movie. It could be laughed off as curious but unreal. But the numbers of readers and viewers should give us pause. A nerve in us is touched, even if we spend little time in airport clubs. Few of us will travel as he travels, and the nature of his goal can seem amusingly odd. Yet author Kirn has tapped something many of us actually share. We are in motion, driven by our own private passions. We are up in the air, in search, between where we began and where we dream of going. Not satisfied with who we are or where we have been, we are pushing for something better, something that makes us real.

> An object in possession seldom retains the same charm that it had in pursuit.
>
> —Pliny the Younger

Some of us are wildly dissatisfied. We imagine more and better, and assume we must go somewhere else and do something new to find what we lack. Some of us are angry and driven to prove we should get what we want. Some of us wrestle with depression, wondering if making any attempt at all could make a difference. Others of us have no particular passion in focus; we simply feel the need to move on because life has to be better in new circumstances. Regardless of our situations, many of us are sure we must get away, move on. The idea has magical appeal.

A cursory glance at Facebook reveals how many people are in motion. Social media are virtual catalogues of personal travels and pursuits. Over a week or two many "Friends" post pictures and descriptions of their travels. The destinations and the reasons vary. Mary does a "selfie" with her daughter outside a college dormitory. Carol pauses on bike rides to show where she arrived and how far she pedaled. Lou collects beach sunsets. Cory has a fish in hand, often from some remote lake. Woody touts mountain ranges, hopefully with animals in the foreground. George prefers urban skylines, often with dramatic sunlight. The examples could be multiplied. We are a people in motion, intent on charting our progress. This restless drive centers on finding what "speaks" to us, a place and an experience that needs little explanation. When we are there, it makes sense. It is real. Finding it, we bask in it and want to tell the world that we have arrived.

Searching and Finding

It may sound surprising, or distracting, but searching and finding are deeply religious pursuits. They have a long, explicitly religious history. As personal as our journeys seem, the instinct to travel in search is not new; countless people have set forth over thousands of years. To be religious is to seek, and to seek is to be religious, and both mark us as human. We are driven to leave our ordinary circumstances, if only briefly, to find what is real, what will make us whole. More often, such journeys are not brief interludes; they define our lives. We want to reach the life we imagine and to secure a distinct identity for ourselves. We are not satisfied with what is; we dream of what could be. So we look beyond ourselves to find ourselves and to secure a life that is not yet ours. Our longing marks this pursuit as religious.

But our naturally good instinct can falter, or even diminish us. There is nothing wrong with earning one million frequent flyer miles. We might envy the travel such an accumulation would allow. But Ryan Bingham's downfall centers on his obsessive, insensitive, and superficial approach to life. Though this is fiction, his example should give us pause. He is consumed by himself. He lives in an insulated, self-constructed world where other people are means to his ends, otherwise they are ignored. Bingham lacks moral or spiritual character. His life is the journey. But his travel demeans people, even himself.

More than ever, our journeys are defined by private intentions. Even in public space, devising the latest text or tweet or posting can absorb us. We are alone in the midst of throngs of people, many pecking away on their own devices. We can be connected instantly, but our most profound selves remain hidden amid flurries of information exchange. Alarmingly, we lose touch with ourselves in the relentless stream. It becomes easy to ignore the important questions: where are we going and how do we propose to get there, and what is the reality of our imaginings? It appears we are going somewhere because we are rushing from point to point. We travel all the time, if only in our imaginations. But where are we going? If we actually get there, what will life be like? Will it resemble what we imagine? Our journeys define us. But will they bring us life?

How do we distinguish worthwhile destinations and the journeys they entail? Of course, not all of our travels must be profound or life-changing. Some days we just need a break to run errands or pursue a hobby or to collapse in a good chair. Some weeks we are ready for vacation and the plans need not be elaborate. Getting away, stepping out of the routine, doesn't require explanation. Nevertheless, even basic time away, a personal Sabbath, has a religious dimension. Even basic travel, which we take for granted, points us toward the legacy of Christian pilgrimage.

> Religion points to that area of human experience
> where in one way or another man comes
> upon mystery as a summons to pilgrimage.
>
> —Frederick Buechner

In every religion, devout followers, or just curious people, are drawn to particular places. Some are sites where events that define our faith traditions occurred. Some are places where nature seems to reveal aspects of truth. Other places are where leaders and teachers performed great works that shaped a faith tradition and the community that embodies it. In a few places, such as the north of Spain, which we cited, people have experienced unexpected religious visions. The growth of faith tradition in part is reflected in the journeys people take to such sites. Streams of people are drawn to stand where great people walked and great events occurred. On such ground, more than recalling the past looms; living amid what is real becomes possible. When you stand in such a place, you become part of it, and it reshapes you.

For Christians, where Jesus walked in the "Holy Land" remains central. In the Middle Ages the idea of pilgrimage to places where faith was inspired became an avid pursuit. Of course pilgrims flocked to Jerusalem and Rome as they were able. Over time other shrines and routes to them gained appeal, many of which continue to draw pilgrims. The "Way of St. James," a trek across northern Spain, was an early destination that still commemorates an early follower of Jesus who later served on the Iberian Peninsula. An estimated two hundred thousand people each year follow the path, which is well planned but can take weeks to complete.

As in the Middle Ages, many modern pilgrims continue to travel to Canterbury, England. The practice arose as medieval Christians were drawn to a shrine honoring Thomas Becket, a church leader murdered on orders of the king. The pilgrimage was celebrated by the medieval author Geoffrey Chaucer in *The Canterbury Tales*. He describes the journey of several dozen people, each representative of a typical medieval figure. Along the way each tells a tale to enliven their travel. It becomes more than the path to a destination; in a sense the journey becomes the actual destination. By how they travel together, the pilgrims discover the ideals of faith they pursue. Arrival at Canterbury recedes in significance. The goal of the trek has been found.

It was not an easy journey nor a vacation nor a luxury. Scores of people went, as Allison went to New Mexico. Pilgrims have always sought healing in the midst of suffering, hope amid despair, resolution and reconciliation that were tangible. People today are walking similar paths, though not necessarily on religious pilgrimages. Nevertheless faith is very much at stake. There may be little actual travel, but the journey may demand upheavals of body and mind. Life may be turned upside down. Many people travel across uncharted terrain in pursuit of survival. How and why they travel reveals much about what it means to have faith.

Into the Wild

"It is definitely like a pilgrimage," Pete acknowledges. We are discussing his passion: caving. Pete is not content to visit well-explored caves. He is part of a small group who actively visit and map unexplored caves or uncharted portions of large cave systems. "This is a golden age of caving," he explains. "The technology, especially long-life batteries, allow us to stay underground for a long time." His enthusiasm for every detail bubbles over, but so does caution.

"We go to places no one has ever been. Not just anybody can go there. These are fragile environments." Pete's conservation ethic is apparent. It matches his drive to explore. He is proud to say he has been where no one has previously gone. But the experience has sobered him. "Not only are caves fragile, people are fragile too. There have been accidents. You have to build a team and know what you're doing. You have to build trust, that's the main thing."

Pete insists other cavers have far more passion than his own. "Some of these guys, it's their whole life. They are really dedicated. It's more than conservation or discovery. For them it is their whole community." He goes on to describe the elaborate preparation needed for even the shortest, simplest outing. Going to remote caves far from any town heightens preparation. The effort pays off when unforeseen things happen, as they often do. The journey proves worthwhile, but there is high risk. And the outcome is never clear. There are always moments of discovery.

When we think of pilgrimage we imagine a well-known destination approached by well-mapped paths. We also presume how we will benefit from the journey. We don't like heading into the unknown. We want to know what to expect, otherwise we become hesitant. But at times we have little choice. Life throws us into the wild and we must plunge ahead as best we can. In the process we discover something of the meaning of faith. There are journeys we must take.

Cheryl Strayed's life went into the wild, and not exactly by choice. Her book *Wild: From Lost to Found on the Pacific Crest Trail* was released in 2012 and the film version followed in 2014. Strayed tells the story of her walk along a 2,600-mile trail around the West. After divorce and various personal and family missteps, her life went into a tailspin. When her mother died she resolved to set forth in search of healing. Not ready for much she encountered, she persevered.[35]

That is the message her work conveys. Amid life's challenges, and one's own frailty, Strayed hung in there. In the wild, she was forced to confront her situation, often alone. Yet she did not learn only self-reliance. She met people, a few of whom proved reliably friendly. She kept going and her own rebuilding proceeded. She wasn't stuck; she could act; she could find a better way, including better relations with herself and with others. She returned from the wild a different person, with a story to tell that many have wanted to hear.

Seasons of Faith

As we have interwoven religious themes and people's life stories, the texture of faith has taken shape. Rooted in personal dreams of significant lives, we are like Tantalus, struggling to choose but never quite seeming to reach what we intend. We move ahead when we find wonder and pause to admire it. For many of us this is in nature. People awakening to faith are alert to the natural world in some way. They study nature in search of what they could not find elsewhere. There they learn to appreciate the complexity of life. They sense forces and processes that shatter human presumption. They find possibilities that human beings have done nothing to create but from which they can truly benefit. They learn something of the meaning of participation and of connection. The feeling of receiving a gift is apparent. The experience of awakening is vivid.

In those seasons of life the journey toward faith is clearly focused. We are certain we know what is real and what is meant to be. If we have not found it, we have it in our sights. What we must find to be complete is no mystery. It's just a matter of doing what is necessary. Such a time in life is a gift. Believing and trusting come naturally. We can absorb inconveniences; they will be temporary. The eccentricities in the people around us can be charming. The sun shines and the wind fills our sails. We feel nostalgia being built. There are no obstacles in our way. We are ready to go.

Yet nature in general, and our lives in particular, can be the setting for storms, upheavals, or just gradual erosion. Some days we marvel at life's beauty and celebrate our role in it. Other days clouds gather and we must find shelter. Some days we cherish every moment. Other days we look for ways to blot out what is happening. Most troubling of all, not all clouds lift quickly. New days begin and still there is gloom. We are forced to stagger onward wondering what to do next. When such seasons of life arrive, we don't know what to do or what to believe. What does faith mean then? Where is God, if God is there at all?

> The feeling remains that God is on the journey, too.
>
> —Attributed to Teresa of Ávila

Art wondered where God was as he went driving alone one night. There was no special destination, there were no particular chores. He simply went driving after dark with no intention of studying the scenery. A long country road sufficed; he had no idea when he would return. Of one thing Art was certain: he needed space to figure out what he would do differently in his life.

Nearing his senior year of college, Art had been obsessed with going to law school. The courses he took, the contacts he sought, most of the conversations he had, all quickly revealed his single-minded intention. Even in casual conversations, and certainly in classroom discussion, Art tried to act as he imagined a lawyer would act. Not just any lawyer, for Art envisioned that he would become a high-powered litigator. His demeanor became obnoxious and made him the butt of snickers and mockery, some of which was apparent. Still Art plunged ahead, outwardly assertive, inwardly trying to convince himself that he had figured out life. He was sure that he was destined to be a great lawyer. Then they won't laugh, he reassured himself.

There was no single moment Art could pinpoint. Rather, there was a gradual realization: he would not go to law school and he would not become a lawyer. It had little to do with his grades. Art had done well enough to keep his fantasy inflated. But two thoughts slowly crept into Art's awareness. First, he really didn't want to be a lawyer. He hadn't been entirely sure what they did other than try cases and be interviewed on television. The more he learned about the profession the less it seemed like a fit. He had imagined himself to be a lawyer, but it was only imagination. His abilities and energies lay elsewhere.

Second, even more sobering, Art had created an image of being a lawyer in a vain effort to feel good about himself. The bluster and the assertiveness masked grave doubt. This was a poor effort to solve the problem of self-esteem. As he realized that being a lawyer would not be in his future, Art was compelled to look deeply at himself. As he lost the sense of control he had tried to muster, he did not like what he saw. His life seemed a mass of insecurity and uncertainty. He had tried to validate himself by what appearances he could muster. Now his dream was dying and he had to look within. Seeking space to find focus, he went for a long drive.

At various points in our lives, we are confronted by the reality of loss. It happens in ways we foresee, such as the end of a phase of life and the start of a new one. Graduation, marriage, and other rites of passage are welcome, even though they signal the end of a phase of life. But loss comes in many forms. Disagreements lead to alienation, breaking apart families and friendships. Or people simply drift apart, eventually realizing that a once vital connection has ended unceremoniously. Jobs also come and go, more often in unwelcome than welcome ways. Nagging health issues can linger unresolved, then turn chronic and even disabling. Loss comes upon us in various ways, but all are deeply personal, striking at our confidence and our hope. What we believed in, perhaps without much question, proves fragile and breaks apart.

Then we feel the reality of loss painfully. Loss hits us with unpredictable force. We are never prepared; we are not at all sure what it would mean to be "ready" for such an experience. Above all, we feel the loss of control over our lives, and we are stunned. We are forced to take journeys we never imagined, like setting out in a car not knowing where we are going or when we will return. At its worst, the world feels shattered, and we don't know if we can do anything to put it back together. At such times, when there seems so little to hold onto, faith can mean little, and God even less.

Amid loss we are apt to feel only absence. There is a hole where something or someone that once helped to define who we are now has gone. The pain of loss is the grim realization that we cannot recapture life as it once was. We cannot go back to the self we were before there was a void into which we fell. The self we thought we were going to be has faded away. The self we might be has become uncertain. For a time we are stamped by loss and little else. If we think of it at all, we wonder how we go forward, or even what that means. As Robert Southey wrote, "Time may heal the anguish of the wound, but the loss cannot be repaired."[36] We will never be quite the same. So how, after the experience of loss, can we have faith, and why should we?

With the death of a loved one being the most profound loss, we can chart our reaction. It is now clear that grief is a process consisting of five stages:

- Denial

- Anger

- Bargaining

- Depression

- Acceptance

It should be clear that grief is predictable and unavoidable.[37] If we try to avoid this natural pattern of response to loss, we risk prolonging the experience. Worse, we risk becoming stuck at one stage or another, especially denial or anger. Regardless of how we assume we should feel, or any expectation of somehow being in control of ourselves and the situation, the grief response unfolds. If we allow ourselves to live into the experience, it will carry us forward, toward a place of acceptance. At the time, what acceptance means for us can seem too abstract and remote.

In the midst of loss we seek explanation and recovery. Once we can no longer deny what has occurred, our anger and our bargaining kick in. Trying to exercise control, but clearly losing it, we vainly focus on rebuilding what was shattered, on some manner of restitution. That can never truly be. We must move to a new place, a different life, without knowing what that means.

Jack only speaks of recovery from serious illness in cautious terms. After weeks in hospitals and rehab facilities, he is better. In that sense much of his physical ability has returned and his mind again is sharp. He is alert enough now to chart stages of illness and recovery over a lengthy period of time. At first, in the depth of illness, he was only barely aware. As recovery began, a seed burst forth, Jack says. He became aware again gradually. As he did, two realizations became prominent. First, he realized that he wanted to live, he wanted to be alive fully again. Then he felt a presence beyond himself, that he must sort out for some time. In that sense, Jack's experience is like the progression of grief. Jack knows something has been lost and something else has been gained. He can never return to the life he once enjoyed. But like grief, he can track his movement toward a sense of acceptance. Even more, he speaks of healing as something other than physical return to a prior state. Jack is intent on moving forward, knowing that entails a new, different life. He is discovering the meaning of healing, and of faith.

Ironically, given health challenges that have curtailed much of his activity, Jack has felt empowered. He can no longer play tennis, a sport in which he excelled. He is long retired from work and from volunteer activities. But the energies that once defined much of his life are applied in other pursuits, especially in writing poetry. The determination to win, and the enjoyment of the pursuit, have been recast. So Jack has adapted to a situation he never would have chosen. But he has made creative choices and so proven the depth of his faith. As we have emphasized, and as Jack has shown, the essence of faith is making choices that lead to a life of significance. But how exactly can this happen?

> Things which matter most must never be
> at the mercy of things which matter least.
>
> —Attributed to Johann Wolfgang von Goethe

How Can We Know the Way?

Whether we speak of grief or healing or Jack's interpretation of them, what we are describing is the most profound journey of all. It can be a pilgrimage, even if our location never shifts. Physical movement can be incidental to the process. It is a journey of the soul. What can make it a pilgrimage is that we can be transformed long before we reach any destination. Healing, the recovery of our bodies and our souls, becomes a pilgrimage during which we can become renewed people, made new because we become whole.

Of course it is not as easy or clear or obvious as it sounds. Healing and recovery indeed mean that we are in some sense restored. But, as this description implies, being restored does not mean repealing all that has happened, or returning to a prior innocence. Jack cannot go back, he must go forward. We want to suggest what this means.

Our bodies and our souls have an incredible ability to rebuild from trauma. Nevertheless, healing may leave us with scars. Some scars are visible, such as the thin line on a leg that shows a knee has been replaced. Healing and a return to physical ability have occurred and the process has left a mark. By analogy, also apparent, trauma can leave emotional scars. Stung by painful experience, we turn protective, fearful of more hurt, resentful of what has occurred. Our capacity for trust has been damaged, as we shall grasp. Faith becomes a goal too far to reach, given our preoccupation and mistrust. The vulnerability faith requires may be too much of a risk. Yet we wrestle with it. We want to believe again. We want to trust again. But we cannot do so in the old way. We must build a new kind of trust, and journey toward faith along a different path.

Illness and emotional trauma are journeys we never intended. But they can become true pilgrimages, as Jack discovered. A sprout of new life can appear. God can be discovered and the will to live can resurface in an entirely new form. Healing and recovery chart a new path, a way that brings unforeseen possibility. In his recovery, Jack reported a sense of unforeseen connection beyond himself, though not in accustomed ways. In the midst of this journey, he inexplicably saw beyond himself. The experience was his own, but he moved beyond the lure of isolation. There was a feeling of more, of being with, and of moving toward greater realization. He could see into his situation and then beneath its surface. There was a reassuring presence in the midst of it.

In several of his recent works, the English philosopher Roger Scruton has challenged the notion that nothing lies beneath the surface of momentary, sensory experience, nor of our mental reflections. Scruton's task is to confront atheism, which he sees as a self-centered turn away from responsibility to others. To make this case, Scruton taps several Jewish philosophers, Emmanuel Levinas and Martin Buber, to consider the idea that human experiences point beyond themselves.

Science, the refuge of atheists, is inadequate as a source of comprehensive insight. Science cannot explain human freedom, especially the freedom to make choices, Scruton maintains. Nor can science explain, or motivate, human responsibility. Ethical principles and the behaviors they prompt transcend scientific, rational thinking. Science is a mode of explanation and a basis for quantifiable exploration. By nature it stands apart in principled objectivity.[38]

But human experiences, especially those of circumstances and of encounters with others, are as much subjective as they are objective. Faith begins at the point of seeing beyond, within, and beneath what we experience, and not simply in terms of mechanical explanations. Faith begins where we "see" others. Scruton is especially focused on the human face as figurative of the perceptions he considers. In the faces of people or of nature, the sacred is manifest. There is a sense of God's presence that opens up to us in daily experience. It comes to us as a gift. Even more, as Jack's experience unveils, once we see, we are invited to follow. What we glimpse is the beginning of a path, a way forward, where none had been apparent before.

The notion of a way forward, or finding "the" way, or being led along a path toward truth, is prominent in Christianity. A key reference in the New Testament is found in John's gospel, chapter 14, verses 1–6:

> "Do not let your hearts be troubled. Believe in God, believe also in me. In my Father's house there are many dwelling places. If it were not so, would I have told you that I go to prepare a place for you? And if I go and prepare a place for you, I will come again and will take you to myself, so that where I am, there you may be also. And you know the way to the place where I am going." Thomas said to him, "Lord, we do not know where you are going. How can we know the way?" Jesus said to him, "I am the way, and the truth, and the life. No one comes to the Father except through me."

This passage is at once troubling and reassuring. It touches our own, contemporary questions in the form of Thomas's inquiry. "How can we know the way?" There may be no more nagging question for countless people now. Further, the passage begins on a very welcome note: "In my Father's house there are many dwelling places." There is a breathtaking, expansive sense of welcome for people on different journeys, people seeking to turn their wanderings through life into pilgrimages that tap deep, substantive issues and lead us to a better place. Jesus is describing, and in a sense actually embodies, a way for us to follow, a way for us to live truly. For Christians, this is the "good news." This is how the Christian message is often described. "Good news" is the essence of Christianity.

> The church is constituted as a new people
> who have been gathered from the nations to
> remind the world that we are in fact one people.
>
> —Stanley Hauerwas
> *In Good Company: The Church as Polis*

But the latter part of the same passage raises red flags for many people. "No one comes to the Father except through me." This sentence appears to signal that Christianity is unequivocally exclusive. "Many dwelling places" appears overshadowed by one way, and only one way. That case is being made by some influential voices in Christian circles. Ideas and ways of thinking far removed from the message of the New Testament have been conflated with Jesus's words. It can be made to seem that unless one "accepts Christ as one's personal savior," in a decisive moment of religious conversion, then one is doomed to suffer eternal damnation. The threat is profound and has troubled people for centuries. The assurance that resonates through John 14 can also be turned into false pride, even religious arrogance, and certainly exclusivity. Instances of horrific abuse, particularly of Jewish people, have resulted.

It should be noted that Jesus has profound appeal and respect beyond Christian circles. His life and his words exert wide appeal, and are not read in exclusive terms. It should also be apparent that numerous Christians, likely a clear majority of the more than two billion, do not apply Jesus's words as an exclusive claim and certainly not as legitimating discrimination or abuse of those whose religious paths take different form and lead in other directions. The core message of Jesus, especially "love of God and love of neighbor," align beautifully with the other major religions. These words counsel only welcome to people on various journeys, in diverse circumstances, toward other envisioned destinations. There is no sense of one way versus another way, nor any sense that exclusivity and judgment are the norms. The larger message and life of Jesus point toward a broad sense of welcome.

We emphasize that Christianity, following in the way of Jesus, offers respect and affirmation of all people seeking to find a way. A closer look at Jesus's words in John 14 brings this to light. For one thing, as author Brian McLaren explains, Thomas's question of how to "know" is somewhat misleading. We assume "knowing" means information or a technical and prescriptive answer to our question. We want the words of Jesus to tell us what to do. Knowing in this sense means following, being in the presence of, living into the example of Jesus. Jesus rises as a guide, pointing toward a path, a way that we may take toward life we never imagined, and perhaps never intended. To follow the way, in other words, is to invest ourselves deeply in it, to follow where it leads, becoming transformed in our lives as we go along. We make it our own.

Second, as McLaren implies, the way of Jesus and those who have followed him toward God is distinctive, and raise up a distinctive community and shared as well as personal identity. Identity means particularity. As Christians, the authors of this book are called to live in certain ways, to uphold certain ideals, to embody certain values. Identity must have definition, must be set apart, must be readily recognizable. We style our journey through life in this way, and, as has been suggested, find that a journey becomes a pilgrimage.[39]

Being distinctive and being exclusive are not the same thing; they are entirely different. Christianity, and the way of life to which it invites people, has a particular cast, a shape and a direction. As Christians, we affirm the distinctive truth we find in Jesus Christ as embodiment of divine love. We also affirm the intention of the Christian church to be the living witness to the life of Jesus and the model of human society as well as the anticipation of God's eternal realm beyond this physical life. Yet such a confession of faith could easily be read as a statement of Christian exclusivity and pretense. Indeed, a robustly confessional tone has surfaced over the centuries in Christian mission, in the church's accommodation to cultural as well as political imperialism, and in outright instances of oppression, notably slavery.

> Too much of anything is dangerous unless it's God's Love.
>
> —Reign

We take a decidedly different tack. We believe genuine affirmation of Christianity's core tenets—love of God and love of neighbor—requires followers of Jesus Christ to work for justice and reconciliation among all people. In Jesus, we see one who welcomed and honored all who came in faith, notably the ill and outcast. We maintain that when Christians move deeply and openly into their own faith, they unearth a basis for honoring all people and their faiths.

In various ways, but especially in emphasizing love of God and love of neighbor, the essence of Christianity resonates with the principles of other faiths. We see in Jesus a gathering point for many on their pilgrimages, though not always the end point. We arrive, then, as the Jesus whom Mohandas Gandhi, a Hindu, could affirm. We place the emphasis on reaching natural meeting points, not points of exclusivity and divergence. We also acknowledge, humbly, that the world's two billion Christians are hardly of like mind on many theological and practical matters. Indeed, we represent two expressions of Christian tradition. But rather than allow ourselves to be divided, we have found abundant points of common affirmation. We witness to the ideal that what unites us is more compelling and abundant than what could divide us.

But in the face of such variety, and even divergence, how could one's journey through life gain sufficient focus and direction to become a lasting pilgrimage in faith? How can we stay on the path, and name it as our way? Our pilgrimage toward faith in this book now turns to the question of what lasts and, in the most personal sense, what can we trust?

A Question to Consider Where is your thin place, that "place where the space between heaven and earth collapses, where the walls weaken and another dimension seems nearer than usual"?

A Thing You Can Do It has been said that if you know only one religious tradition, you know none. As part of your spiritual pilgrimage, choose one of the world's religions and learn more about it through a book, a lecture, or a class.

CHAPTER 4

The Faith to Live Differently

> Everyone thinks of changing the world,
> but no one thinks of changing himself [or herself].
>
> —Leo Tolstoy

When I (Michael) was first married, we lived in Holland, Michigan. It's probably no surprise that it had a considerable Dutch influence. There is a wooden shoe factory, Dutch architecture, and tulips everywhere. One evening my wife and I decided to visit the quaint replica of a Dutch village. We discovered that it had a few carnival rides and decided to try the circling swings. It was a quiet evening so we were the only ones on the ride. We strapped ourselves into the seats side by side, and then the giant circle began to rise and the swings began to twirl round and round. Higher and higher we went.

It began as a wonderful experience for newlyweds. But while we were circling in the sky, the operator wandered off. I can't say for sure how long he was away, but it felt like fifteen to twenty minutes. In the beginning it was fun. We had the sensation of flying and a great view of the landscape around us. But as time passed, it became incredibly boring. We just kept circling and seeing the same thing over and over. We tried to get the operator's attention, but he was too far away. Boredom turned into motion sickness, but there was nothing we could do to stop the ride. Finally, the operator casually wandered back and we were saved!

As we think about this experience we realize that for many, life can be like this. We begin new careers, enter into new relationships, and relocate to new places. It's fun at first. But after a while, it feels like we are circling round and round, seeing the same things over and over, with no end in sight. It's hard to break this cycle when we live every day exactly like we lived yesterday.

Many of us are stuck and we don't know how to change. How many of us go to bed thinking that tomorrow we'll start eating healthier, tomorrow we'll start exercising, tomorrow we'll come home early to be with family, tomorrow we'll make prayer a part of our day, or tomorrow we'll call that family member we've neglected? But then we get up and live tomorrow exactly like we did yesterday. Honestly, if we did everything tomorrow that we committed to changing today, we'd be awesome! But all too often we don't change.

In a Religious Rut

In previous chapters we've spoken of awakening to wonder and the pilgrimage to faith. Many of us yearn to experience these things and move in a new direction, but no matter what we do,

our pilgrimage ends up following the same path we've been plod-
ding most of our lives. We are stuck in a religious rut, unable to
break free from it and move in a new direction.

Being stuck in a religious rut is not a new phenomenon. As
the book of James in scripture describes, a question is raised to
help people move out of their religious ruts, and it is as relevant
and penetrating today as it was two thousand years ago. The
question is, "Can faith save you?" At its heart, it is asking us to
consider whether we are living into God's dream for what creation
can be, for what we can be. Will we be saved from living a life
that doesn't avail itself of all that God offers us? The hope of faith
is that it can indeed save us and help us make choices that lead to
a life of significance.

This question isn't intended to be a hypothetical question
about what's possible in the future. It is really asking if our faith
is saving us today. Is faith helping us live differently? An honest
answer from many may be "no." It's not because of a lack of
desire. We desperately want to live differently. But we are stuck
in a rut, and our approach to faith doesn't seem to help us get
unstuck.

This can be difficult for people to talk about. Steve recently
visited his pastor. He had mentioned for some time that he wanted
to meet, but he was very hesitant to explain why. He had grown
up in a church and was well versed in the sacred sources of the
faith, but there was uneasiness in speaking about things spiritual. After nearly an hour of dancing around the topic, he finally
said, "Here's the thing. I don't know if I can still call myself a
Christian. I don't know what I believe or if I believe anything. I
even question whether any of this makes a difference." His fear
in admitting this was that he may no longer be welcome in the
church, a community he loved.

He's not alone. There are many who believe that if they
shared what they truly believe, or don't believe, the church would

reject them. If you're wondering this too, you're not alone. It may help to understand why so many of us struggle with the idea of faith today.

Faith—Getting It Right or Getting It Lived?

Much of our modern-day emphasis on faith has been about getting it right—believing the right doctrines and having the right dogmas. And this was predicated on the belief that what these things described existed and could be known. We now live in a time when there has been an erosion of confidence that the words and ideas used to express the Christian faith have any connection to what is real.

It used to be that people embraced religious truth as true for all people, at all times and in all places. Now truth is more personal in nature. If people express belief in the tenets of faith, it is usually qualified as true "for me." We spoke of the beginnings of this turn in *A Church Beyond Belief* as what is termed a "hedged orthodoxy." This means that when someone affirms traditional Christian beliefs, they are increasingly reticent to say that Christian beliefs are true for all people. Therefore they hedge the affirmation of their beliefs by adding that it is true "for me." Stephen Colbert coined this "truthiness." The truthiness of something isn't about facts. It's about what you feel in your gut!

At its core, this means we are questioning whether religious ideas like the Atonement, hell, and the Trinity really exist. These are the things that have been handed down to us as the substance of faith. Today, we increasingly view them as ideas that were believable in the past, but modern sensibilities make them hard to accept today. We treat them as antiquated views that don't mesh well with contemporary understanding. Because of this, we feel free to reject the words of our tradition or inject new meaning into them so that they have personal relevance for us.

We saw this shift in understanding begin when a bright and entrepreneurial young man dropped out of a prestigious university to pursue his ideas in science and technology. We all know his name today because his inventions and innovations have forever changed the way we live and see the world. We are not speaking of Bill Gates, Steve Jobs, or Mark Zuckerberg. He is the seventeenth-century Renaissance man Galileo.

Through his discoveries he prompted many to begin questioning what is real and what is true. Through Galileo's innovations of the telescope, he demonstrated that the earth revolves around the sun, challenging religious dogma that saw the earth at the center of the universe. He also helped develop the microscope, allowing people to see reality at a level of detail that was not possible before this. People began to see that what they thought was true doesn't always correspond with reality.

This realization was so profound that Galileo began to question whether there is a reality beyond what we construct in our minds. Galileo's ideas proved to be too progressive for the church. Faith was not about questioning long-held doctrines. It was about affirming what had been handed down. The result was that Galileo was called upon to recant his beliefs and sentenced to spend the remainder of his life, nearly a decade, under house arrest.

Today, we are able to affirm Galileo's discoveries and the questions he raised about reality. And unlike Galileo, we are free to explore the meaning of faith without being subject to house arrest! We have the ability to wonder whether the "God talk" we use reflects reality.

The Apostles' Creed

I believe in God, the Father almighty,
    creator of heaven and earth.
I believe in Jesus Christ, his only Son, our Lord.

> He was conceived by the Holy Spirit,
>> and born of the Virgin Mary.
> He suffered under Pontius Pilate,
>> was crucified, died, and was buried.
> He descended to the dead.
> On the third day he rose again.
> He ascended into heaven,
>> and is seated at the right hand of the Father,
> He will come again to judge the living and the dead.
> I believe in the Holy Spirit,
>> the holy catholic Church,
>> the communion of saints,
>> the forgiveness of sins,
>> the resurrection of the body,
>> and the life everlasting. Amen

This was made clear when one of us was coleading a class on the Apostles' Creed. We began by asking people to rewrite the creed in a way that would be more understandable and meaningful for people today. Not long ago, people would have felt constrained to restate the inherited meaning so it would be easier to understand for a contemporary audience. This class felt no such restraint. Instead, they felt free to use the terms as a launching pad to explore meanings that may have a personal relevance to them. The words weren't bound by a reality they described. Everyone felt the freedom to inject new meanings or to flat out reject terms or concepts as irrelevant.

This may seem a slippery slope when it comes to beliefs, but it is the state of where many people are. If any community of faith wants to be a place where people can explore faith, then they had better be prepared for people to ask questions, express skepticism, and have grave doubts—all of which are essential in the pursuit of a real, authentic faith.

The difficulty is that this skepticism leaves us wondering if the Christian faith has anything to offer us. Can faith save us? Can it help us live differently?

It may help us to think of faith as the quest of getting it lived, not about getting it right.[40] The substance of faith does not reside in our heads. It resides in our lives. It is what fuels our passion and motivates us to action. It is what gives us the confidence to make courageous choices and hard decisions, all of which help us live into the fullness of who God created us to be and do what God created us to do.

This is precisely the point of the question posed in James, "Can faith save you?" Just prior to this, James asks, "What good is it, my brothers and sisters, if you say you have faith but do not have works?" (James 2:14a). The problem was that people were using the words of faith, but they were not living it. And James puts it quite bluntly, a faith that is not lived is dead. Basically, James says that if people really believed in Jesus and the God to whom Jesus's life points, they then would be different because they are living differently. Faith would help them have the courage to make the choices that lead to a different kind of life, one of greater significance.

Trust: A New Way of Seeing Faith

When I (Michael) was in Cairo, late one night I took a walk. I had been traveling with a group and needed a little space. Somehow, and I'm not sure how this happened, I ended up opposite my hotel on a very busy street. It had five lanes of traffic heading each direction, and it was so busy that there was never a break in traffic to get across the road. To complicate things, many of the cars didn't use their headlights in the belief that this would help with their gas mileage. I don't know whether that actually works, but I do know it doesn't help pedestrians at night!

As I stood there, an Egyptian man looked at me and pointed across the road, as if to say, "Do you need to get to the other side?" I nodded yes. Then with sympathetic eyes, he held out his hand. I walked over to him and placed my hand in his. Then he turned and started to walk across the road, with me in tow like a little child. Cars honked, swerved, and screeched as we walked across the street. Because I lived to write about this, you know that I made it to the other side.

I'm not sure what made me trust that man in that moment. I guess Hemingway was right: "The best way to find out if you can trust somebody is to trust them." It wasn't easy, especially being strangers. But it reminded me of what it means to trust. Trust didn't give me certainty that I would get to the other side—at times I felt I was being dragged! Trust did not give me a complete calm that all would be okay—I had sweaty palms, shortness of breath, and high anxiety. Too often we think that trust in God eliminates these things, but it often does not. Trust is what allows us to move in a new direction that we couldn't have gone by ourselves. It is through trust that we are released to live differently. Conversely, when we lack trust, we lack the ability to change.

> To have faith is to trust yourself to the water.
> When you swim you don't grab hold of the water,
> because if you do you will sink and drown.
> Instead you relax, and float.
>
> —Alan W. Watts

There is a sense in which our sacred source of faith, the Bible, is about the journey of trusting in God. We see in the

Old Testament that the Israelites had trust issues. It tells of their journey from Egypt to the Promised Land. It's not a story that narrates history. It is a story about what trust, or lack thereof, means in the journey of faith.

The Israelites were slaves in Egypt, and through Moses's leadership and God's guidance they were able to escape and make their way to a new life in a new place. Like all stories with happy endings, there is a problem along the way.

In making the journey, they quickly discovered it was not an easy trip and rationing food was not fun. So they begin to complain. They cried out, "If only we had died by the hand of the LORD in the land of Egypt, when we sat by the fleshpots and ate our fill of bread; for you have brought us out into this wilderness to kill this whole assembly with hunger" (Exod. 16:3). This is clearly an exaggeration. At that time, slaves received the absolute minimum needed to keep them alive.

> Nobody can go back and start a new beginning,
> but anyone can start today and make a new ending.
>
> —Maria Robinson

God, being gracious, said to Moses (paraphrasing), "Here's what I'm going to do. I'm going to rain down bread on them every morning so that they're able to eat their fill." Sure enough, the next morning there is a bread-like substance on the ground, which they call "manna." The instructions were to collect just enough for the day. However, people being people, some collected much more than they needed and tried to hoard it so they had an excess supply. They quickly found that the excess would spoil before they could eat it. And there were a few good souls who took less than they needed to make sure that everybody had some. Their supply never seemed to run out.

The Israelites didn't trust that they would have food the next day. They did not trust that they could make it to the Promised Land. They did not trust that Moses or God would be with them and guide them to freedom. Instead, for the next forty years they would wandered in the wilderness. It's like they stayed on the carnival ride and circled on the swing round and round, going nowhere in life.

This is not just a story about the Israelites. It is a story about us. It tells us that when we lack trust in something larger than ourselves, we lose the faith that things can be different. Therefore we accept that the way things are is the way they will always be. However, when we trust in God we develop an expectation, a hope, that things can be different. And this allows us to take the first step into a changed life.

In God We Trust

With trust being central to the story of faith, we move to the New Testament and read the stories of Jesus afresh. Let's look at a scene from Jesus's ministry when he is near rock-star status.

Jesus is nearing his height of popularity and has just performed two miracles. The first was the feeding of the five thousand. Crowds had gathered to learn from Jesus, and as they followed him the question arose, "How do we feed this crowd while they're with us?" No problem. A boy has five loaves of bread and two fish. Jesus takes these and, after giving thanks, he begins to share them with the crowd. Miraculously, everyone is able to eat until full—and there are even leftovers.

After all of this teaching and miracle performing, Jesus needs a break and leaves the crowd. But rather than taking a boat, he does it "Jesus style" and walks on water. Another pretty spectacular miracle! The crowds finally catch up to him. But what's interesting is that they're not hot in pursuit of him because of the miracles. They are there because they want more bread! Because of their lack of trust that they'll have food the next day, they miss the big picture of what's possible.

We then come to one of the famous lines of the Bible. Jesus says to them,

"Do not work for the food that perishes, but for the food that endures for eternal life, which the Son of Man will give you" (John 6:27a).

This isn't a lesson that we shouldn't worry about today but instead should focus on getting to heaven. When Jesus uses the phrase "eternal life," he's speaking about the here and now: "'Eternal life' does not speak of immortality or a future life in heaven, but is a metaphor for living now in the unending presence of God."[41] It is about the realm of God that is in our midst. It's about living in the fullness of what God offers us in this day.

Upon hearing this, they wanted to know what they had to do to obtain "eternal life." He then gives them the answer. He draws them in close and tells them: To live this kind of life, the one about which I am speaking, you must "believe in him whom he has sent" (John 6:29). Jesus is asking them to believe in him and in the God who sent him. Jesus is not asking them to believe something about him. The Greek word used for "believe" means "to trust." Jesus is asking them to trust God.

At the heart of everything is trust. But it's not about trusting ourselves or our inner potential. It calls us to look beyond ourselves to God. It asks us to trust that the realm of God is real. Trusting in God stands at the center of what it means to be a person whose life is empowered through faith to live differently. It is through trust that we open ourselves to the mystical and manifold ways that God moves us to new places.

> Don't let your hearts be troubled.
> Trust in God, and trust also in me.
>
> —Jesus Christ
> John 14:1 NLT

We recognize that for many raised in the church, "trusting God" was presented as the solution to any question. If we didn't know what to do, just trust in God to lead us to a decision. If we found ourselves in a mess, just trust in God to help us clean it up. Whatever we faced, just trust in God to help us find a way forward. There was a sense in which "trusting God" was an exhortation to "keep the faith" when the evidence of God was scant in the circumstances in which we found ourselves. It served as a religious equivalent to the idea that it will all work out in the end.

From the perspective of faith, trusting in God is meant to be more than words of encouragement. These words ask something of us. They are a call to action. To trust God is to do something that opens the possibility of a new reality in our relationship with the divine. To open our lives to these possibilities, our spiritual journeys must include two essential elements: looking back and letting go.

Looking Back

The old saying goes, "Hindsight is 20/20." It's easy to look back and know what we should have done. It's easy to know today that we should have bought Apple stock when it went public in 1980. When we look in the rearview mirror at our lives, we see things with a clarity that is not possible when we look to the future.

The same holds true when we look for God in our lives. It's much easier to look back and see God's presence than it is to know what it will look like in the future. Yet rarely do we look back and ask ourselves, "Where was God in this?" We tend to pride ourselves on being forward-looking, never dwelling on the past. In doing so, we're missing an opportunity to see where God has been present. We've forgotten those moments when we were awakened by wonder. We've forgotten the thin places where we were swept up into the realm of something much larger than ourselves. To look only to the future and forget the past creates a spiritual amnesia that weakens our ability to trust God in the present.

As we look back, we sense transcendent moments when something beyond us guided us. Some label this "something" God or Jesus, while others have no label other than a sense of something or someone larger than themselves. Whatever we call these experiences, they are significant moments of spiritual connection to the divine. Rather than forget them or vaguely remember them as a series of "one-off" spiritual experiences, to recall and connect them with one another creates a cumulative spiritual force. We begin to see the story of God in our lives as we recount and embrace what we have experienced in the past.

When we take the time to look back, we are rooting ourselves in the reality of God. It is out of this that we develop the confidence and hope that God will be present in our future. We don't know *how* God will be present; we just trust *that* God will be present. Sometimes, being able to trust *that* God will be present is the difference between giving up or going forward.

Letting Go

Looking back is but one part in learning to trust in God. There is another critical movement in trusting God: letting go and recognizing that we're not in control.

Anyone who has experienced the 12-step program, or watched the transformation of someone who has gone through it, realizes the power of opening our lives to God. It begins at the place many of us find ourselves. We wake up each morning and do the same things over and over, living the same way day after day. And worse yet, we continue even when the pattern of life we follow is not leading us where we want to be. Regardless of any regrets we have and commitments we've made to live differently, we find we do not have the power to change ourselves. To acknowledge this is to admit we are not in control, and we cannot change through shear willpower alone. If that were possible, change would have happened long ago.

Once we admit this, we are ready to turn to a Power outside ourselves. In the 12-step program, it is posed in this way:

> We needed to ask ourselves but one short question. "Do I now believe, or am I even willing to believe, that there is a Power greater than myself?" As soon as one can say that he or she does believe, or is willing to believe, we emphatically assure them that they are on their way. It has been repeatedly proven among us that upon this simple cornerstone a wonderfully effective spiritual structure can be built.[42]

The cornerstone is the ability to trust, that is, "believe" in a Power greater than ourselves. We don't know why this works or how it works. Just that it does.

It's hard for us to admit we're not in control or that we can't do it on our own. We are taught to be independent self-starters whose aim is to accumulate personal accomplishments. This creates the myth that we can be self-made people. The truth is that we have always depended upon others, and circumstances beyond our control have directed our path. No one is self-made. Some exert more influence than others on the course of their lives, but no one is in total control. Turning to a Higher Power for help releases us from the illusion that we are in complete control. It is what opens the door to change.

To let go of control and trust in God can be a difficult step. Yet at the same time it is a freeing one. We no longer have to pretend that we have all the answers. We no longer have to pretend we have it all together. We no longer have to live as if we're going it alone. Letting go of control is what allows us to be real about who we are and where we are in life, and we are finally able to ask for help in finding our way forward. It is what opens the possibility to make different choices and live in different ways.

> God, grant me the serenity
> To accept the things I cannot change,
> Courage to change the things I can,
> And wisdom to know the difference.
>
> —The Serenity Prayer

What If "God" Is a Four-Letter Word?

For those who grew up in a church and felt like they were theologically abused or led astray, it's hard to talk about God or a Higher Power without thinking of all the things one has been taught about God.

While on an international flight, I (Michael) was having a wonderfully engaging conversation with the person next to me. It came up that I was a pastor, and initially she seemed impressed that I could be clergy and seem so normal. She asked a few questions about my faith and I mentioned Jesus—what a surprise that he would come up. It was like I flipped a switch within her. She stood up and in a loud tone told me that all of us Christians were alike. I sat calmly, hoping that this wouldn't attract the attention of a flight attendant. Finally, when she gathered herself, she sat down and explained the version of Christianity with which she was raised. Her family had rejected her brother because he was gay, and they did this in their quest to be faithful to what God wants. Then I understood the pain she was experiencing and why any conversation about Christianity was so difficult. For her, faith has not been a source of hope. Therefore, she rejected faith, God, Jesus, and anything else associated with Christianity. It was almost as if she felt called to make certain no one else would experience the pain she and her brother had while growing up—all done in the name of faith.

It is important that we have the space to approach God in a way that is appropriate to each of us. In the 12-step program, how one sees and names one's Higher Power is based on whatever is comfortable for him or her. The only guidelines given are that "this Power be loving, caring and greater than ourselves."[43] This is echoed in scripture, which recounts the experiences of God by those who have waded into the waters of faith long before us. It is from this they proclaim that God is "merciful and gracious, slow to anger, and abounding in steadfast love and faithfulness" (Exod.

34:6). It is a statement that is made by looking at God in the rear-view mirror through what they have experienced. This is where our spiritual journeys are a constant interchange of looking back and letting go. They dance with each other as we seek to be able to trust in God.

It may seem that we are now at a spiritual stalemate for those who struggle with the idea of God. How can they look back and draw upon positive experiences of God when their experiences have been so negative? It is here that it is important to distinguish between the image of God created by others and experiences of the divine that we may have had. As hard as it can be to separate the two, we must recognize that they are not the same thing. For those who have had God's image distorted into a supreme being who is quick to punish and slow to love, it may take time to realize that this image is not God. We must let go of distorted images of God that stand in the way, that prevent us from sifting through our lives and seeing the moments of transcendence that we've had. At first they may not be easy to identify because they've been obfuscated by others' projections of God. But they're there.

As we recall these experiences, it is not as if we move from no trust to 100 percent confidence. We build trust slowly. We need to continue to reflect on our experiences through prayer, medita-tion, worship, study, conversations, reading, walking in nature, and countless other ways. And day by day, our trust grows, our sense of the divine increases, and we live into the realm of God that is all around us.

Trust, Vulnerability, and Community

Too often we assume that once we know the content of faith we will be able to live differently. But it is not the content of faith that changes us. It is when we grow in our trust in God that we find the resolve to make different choices and take different actions. It is not a trust that a predetermined outcome will occur. There are no divine guarantees for how life unfolds. However, though we don't know how or when things will come together, there is a trust that somehow, someway God will help us live into a new place. It is a trust that whatever the outcome, we will grow into who God has created us to be.

At the center of this is learning to love and be loved. Trust increases our ability to be vulnerable and allow others to see us as we really are. And it's only then that we are able to experience what it is to be embraced for who we are, not just what others want us to be.

> The beginning of love is the will to
> let those we love be perfectly themselves, the
> resolution not to twist them to fit our own image.
> If in loving them we do not love what they are,
> but only their potential likeness to ourselves, then
> we do not love them:
> we only love the reflection of ourselves we find in them.
>
> —Thomas Merton
> *No Man Is an Island*

Being human, at times we will say and do the wrong things, weakening the trust we have in one another. It is here that our evolving trust in God helps us respond to others in ways that rebuild trust rather than tearing it down. Through our relationship with God we learn what it means to admit our shortcomings and seek forgiveness. We learn what it means to have someone who never gives up on us. This is the substance of faith that is learned through the journey of trust.

This is no formula for developing trust or for how our faith will grow through it. And it's hard to begin a journey with an unknown destination and with a little-known companion—God. But it only begins after we take a first step . . . and then another . . . and then another. Perhaps that is why Jesus invited people to begin with small steps so they could experience what trust and faith look like in their lives. Rather than tell people they needed complete trust and absolute faith to see any change, he told them that if they had the faith the size of a small seed, they could move mountains (Matt. 17:20). When we look back at our journey of faith, often we will see that there was no one moment that changed everything. It was through a series of small steps—in our choices and actions—that we are able to live differently.

Julie always felt she was an outsider at church. Her behavior certainly didn't help. In her younger years, she was the one who was described as "a handful." In her teenage years, people would say she was "going through a rough patch." And a rough patch it was. She was caught smoking behind the church, caught with marijuana on the youth mission trip, and in constant trouble for the expletives that littered her speech.

When Julie turned eighteen, she dropped out of high school and moved out on her own. With no work experience or an education, she didn't have a steady job. She slept on any sofa available to her. For a while, Julie used whatever wiles she had to get money from her parents, but eventually they cut her off. They suspected that Julie was using the money to get high or drunk—and they were right.

After several years on her own, she reached such a dark, hopeless place that she felt she had no choice but to return home. It was hard for her to make the call to ask if her parents would take her back. When she finally dialed the number and her mother answered, she could hear the hesitancy in her mother's voice, which was to be expected. She had lied and manipulated her parents to extract money from them. After a very long conversation, her parents agreed that she could return home as long as she agreed to some ground rules for family life.

She was surprised how welcoming her parents were after all she had put them through. Though they didn't push their faith on her, eventually she started attending her family's church again. Of course she tried to be as anonymous as possible. After a few months, she was at an evening service, and it was their custom to take prayer requests. Julie had never shared anything in the past, but something moved her to share her prayer request that evening. She thought this would be a wonderful opportunity to thank her family and church for taking her back after all the pain she had caused. The pastor made her way to Julie and placed the microphone in front of her. She struggled to find the words, and then said, "I want to thank you all for being there to help me clear all the shit out of my life." And then she realized what she had just said. How could she swear in the middle of a church service?! In that moment she felt she had demonstrated that she was the same old Julie who caused trouble wherever she went. During the long pause, Julie lowered our head, waiting for the consequences of what she had just said. And then to her amazement, the congregation erupted into applause. As she looked at the people around her, she could not hold back her tears. She realized that though she had turned her back on them, they had never turned their back on her.

To protect Julie's anonymity, some details have been changed, but this is her story of trust and faith. It was through trust that Julie learned what it means to risk being vulnerable. Through her vulnerability she learned what it means to experience belonging and the offer of forgiveness. She experienced what it means to be seen for who she is and know there is a place for her. She learned what it means to love and be loved. It all began with small steps of trust in God and in others. Out of this she developed the faith that she could live differently.

A Question to Consider What are the images of God of which you need to let go so that you can approach God in a new way?

A Thing You Can Do Begin each morning with the Serenity Prayer so that you can let go of control in areas that are preventing you from change.

CHAPTER 5

Things That Last

Immortality Challenged

From ancient times to the present day, people have wanted to live a life that lasts. It's almost as if we're hardwired to want to do something, leave something, or be something that lives beyond our days on this earth. However, we're not always sure how this is achieved, and we struggle with what this means for how we live day to day. The bottom line: many of us are immortality challenged.

Faith speaks powerfully about this, but unfortunately much of our scriptural heritage on eternity and eternal life has been recast as issues about heaven and hell. Its central focus has been on what happens after we die. As we discussed in chapter 4, what is missed in this understanding is that eternal life also focuses on the here and now. It is about learning how to live a life that will last. And in doing so, we also discover what matters most.

Death is not an event in life:
we do not live to experience death.
If we take eternity to mean
not infinite temporal duration but timelessness,
then eternal life belongs to those who live in the present.
Our life has no end in the way in which
our visual field has no limits.

—Ludwig Wittgenstein
Tractatus Logico-Philosophicus, 6.4311

It is important to understand that the concept of eternal life is not otherworldly. It is about the inbreaking of the realm of God into the world in the present. This realm represents that which brings purpose to our lives and guides us toward what matters most. And when we attend to what matters most, who we are and what we do become things that last. Eternity isn't something that begins when we die and go to heaven. Eternity begins today. It begins at the very moment that we live in the realm of God. The embrace of eternal life is to begin seeing the world in a new way and living in a new way. It is to see new possibilities for ourselves and others through the eyes of faith. Eternal life isn't something we wait to receive. It is something we can experience today.

When we understand this, we see that the opposite of eternal life is not death. The opposite of eternal life is a wasted life. It is a life that missed the opportunity to participate in the things that matter most. It is a life relegated to the mundane and monotonous things that never calls forth a greater purpose or draws upon our God-given gifts. Instead of a life filled with meaning and purpose, we simply go through the motions of life, wasting the opportunity to have truly lived.

Erik Erikson developed a theory of our psychosocial development that has had a lasting impact on how we understand the issues we face as we grow and mature. He proposes that we move through eight stages in life. These stages are not based on what we should do. They are based on his study of human development that simply observed that this is the ways things seem to be.

As we consider things that last, the final stage is of particular importance and raises some critical questions. Erikson observed that in our final phase of life, we start asking questions like, Did I live my life to the fullest? Did I accomplish my goals? Do I have any regrets? How we answer these questions determines whether we look back on our lives with a sense of fulfillment or despair. If we believe we have wasted our lives, then we experience depression and regret. But if we believe we lived a life of significance, we experience a sense of satisfaction and integrity about our lives.

The true tragedy is when people never get around to asking these questions. This is why Jesus's concern with eternal life becomes so important. If eternal life is the possibility of entering into the realm of God here and now, then it was "mission critical" for Jesus to raise this possibility for all people. If we're honest with ourselves, we need someone to prompt us to consider whether we're living a life that will last or a life that is fleeting and being wasted.

In Jesus's words about eternal life, the immediacy of what God offers us comes through. In the Gospel of John, Jesus says, "anyone who hears my word and believes him who sent me has eternal life, and does not come under judgment, but has passed from death to life" (5:24). Notice that Jesus doesn't say we "*will* have eternal life," or "*will* pass from death to life." He says one "*has* eternal life" and "*has* passed from death to life." This means that today, right now, in this moment, we can begin to live into the realm of God. And when we do, we begin to build a life around things that last.

This helps us understand why scripture treats this subject with such urgency and intensity. There is much at stake! This also means that now is the time to ask ourselves whether we are focusing on the things that matter most. Today is the day to consider what it means to participate in things that last.

Who I Am vs. Who I Yearn to Be

Scripture has a very high view of human potential that for millennia people have drawn from to elevate the possibilities they see for themselves. In Psalm 8, the author considers our place in this world. The psalmist writes, "When I look at your heavens, the work of your fingers, the moon and the stars that you have established; what are human beings that you are mindful of them, mortals that you care for them? Yet you have made them a little lower than God, and crowned them with glory and honor" (vv. 3–5). This is quite a statement. It moves us toward a view of humanity that sees each person as one whose life is filled with potential meaning and significance.

The truth is that many motivational speakers and self-help books seem to say something quite similar—the whole "you're destined to do great things" kind of approach. But from the perspective of faith, the possibilities are so much deeper and the significance so much greater about the potential meaning of our lives.

If we turn to the beginning of the story of creation, we find the foundation of who we're created to be and what we are created to do. In Genesis 1, God creates the earth and everything in it. As God comes to the pinnacle of creation, humankind arrives on the scene. It says this about humanity "God created humankind in his image, in the image of God he created them" (v. 27). We are created in the image of God. It's hard to have any higher view of humanity than this! However, this doesn't just speak to our value; it also speaks to our ultimate vocation.

To be created in the image of God means that each and every one of us, without exception, is created with the vocation to be "the bearer of the divine presence."[44] We have the opportunity to be used by God to "extend the presence of God from heaven (the cosmic holy of holies) to earth (the holy place)."[45] This presents the possibility that through the lives we lead, God will use us to fill the earth with God's presence and goodness "so that God may be all in all" (1 Cor. 15:28). We are created to share in building things that last.

Juxtaposed against this possibility is the way many of us actually live. We may lack the perspective of faith that awakens us to the potential of each day. We haven't recognized that today is the day in which eternal life can begin. We have yet to realize that today God can use us to extend God's presence in the world. Without faith we're apt to drift through life, not recognizing the possibilities within us and around us.

Jill is twenty-eight and has an undergraduate degree from an elite university. She has bold dreams about what she wants to do and accomplish, but those dreams are slowly fading. She's struggled to find a job in her chosen profession. She has been living with her parents, which really cramps her style, but she can't afford any other option. Fortunately, she's able to bartend on weekends to pay her student loans.

Mark is thirty-three and has been married for four years. He has a very well-paying corporate job and a beautiful home in the 'burbs. Yet with all of this, he feels life is slipping away. He's always wanted to be a teacher and a coach. The problem is that now he can't afford to make a career change. With a large mortgage and plans for children on the horizon, he feels trapped in a job that is sucking the life out of him.

> Psychologists paid college students to do nothing: while their physical needs were met, they were forbidden to work. Within four to eight hours, students became unhappy, even though they earned significantly more money than they could have in other jobs. They needed stimulation and challenge and chose to leave their well-paying "cushy" job for work that was not only more demanding but also less financially rewarding.
>
> —Tal Ben-Shahar
> *Happier: Learn the Secrets*
> *to Daily Joy and Lasting Fulfillment*

Against the backdrop of what's possible, this is where many of us find ourselves. We, like Jill and Mark, are drifting through life. It's not that all parts of our lives are bad. But we are missing that something more. We aren't living lives that last. In fact, we probably hope that they don't last! Many of us are young enough that we believe things will turn around. But at the same time we don't know how to change the trajectory of our lives.

Happiness: An Elusive Goal

Though we may not know how to live differently, we all seem to agree on the goal: happiness. After all, isn't being happy the ultimate goal? If you ask parents their greatest wish for their children, it's usually some form of "I just want them to be happy." Sometimes we quote scripture to support this pursuit. In Psalm 34 it says, "happy are those who take refuge in [God]" (v. 8). This emphasis is understandable because it seems a fundamental human desire to want to be happy. We strive to have jobs that make us happy, live where we are happy, spend time with those who make us happy, and spend our free time doing things that make us happy. Life is one grand pursuit of happiness.

While in Richmond, Virginia, the two of us had the opportunity to do a Segway tour of the city with our spouses. It was great fun! It took us a few minutes to get our "Segway legs," but soon we were zipping around, twirling in circles, and doing a little free-styling when the tour guide wasn't looking. When we finished, we were on an adrenaline high.

As much fun as it was, soon the adrenaline faded and we returned to our usual selves. Though we have very fond memories of this, it's not necessarily something we think about often. And we're certain that if we ever underwent a psychological evaluation to assess our personal wellbeing, we didn't move higher up the scale because of this experience. It's like this with many pursuits. We have great dinners out, wonderful vacations, a great day skiing or mountain biking, but once the experience is over, the emotional high is gone and we count the days until the next time we can do it all over again.

These things represent temporary pleasures that, while fun and uplifting at the time, don't stay with us. It's only during the experience that they elevate our sense of well-being. But once they end, so too does the happiness connected with them.

Tal Ben-Shahar, a leading researcher on happiness, says that the pursuit of pleasure as the path to happiness will always come up short. He recounts an episode of a television series that unfolds like an ancient story teaching us a timeless lesson:

> The gravity of this error [hedonism] is revealed in an old episode of "The Twilight Zone" in which a ruthless criminal, killed while running from the police, is greeted by an angel sent to

grant his every wish. The man, fully aware of his life of crime, cannot believe that he is in heaven. He is initially baffled but then accepts his good fortune and begins to list his desires: he asks for an obscene sum of money and receives it; he asks for his favorite food and it is served to him; he asks for beautiful women and they appear. Life (after death), it seems, could not be better. However, as time goes by, the pleasure he derives from continuous indulgence begins to diminish; the effortlessness of his existence becomes tiresome. He asks the angel for some work that will challenge him and is told that in this place he can get whatever he wants —except the chance to work for the things he receives. Without any challenges, the criminal becomes increasingly frustrated. Finally, in utter desperation, he says to the angel that he wants to get out, to go to "the other place." The criminal, assuming that he is in heaven, wants to go to hell. The camera zooms in on the angel as his delicate face turns devious and threatening. With the ominous laughter of the devil, he says, "This is the other place."[46]

Even with such cautionary tales, some of us think we can beat the odds. But none of us ever do.

It's here that faith redirects us in our quest for happiness. Our faith tradition informs us that happiness is not the goal. It is the byproduct that occurs when we focus on the things that matter most. In the Gospel of Matthew, Jesus offers these words to people who are worried about getting what they want out of life: "But strive first for the kingdom of God and his righteousness, and all these things will be given to you as well" (Matt. 6:33). In more common parlance, when we focus on what matters most, we have what we hope to have and become who we yearn to be.

> The idea that one more dollar, one more dalliance, one more rung on the ladder will make us feel sated reflects a misunderstanding about human nature—a misunderstanding which is built into human nature; that we are designed to feel that the next great goal will bring bliss, and the bliss is designed to evaporate shortly after we get there.
>
> —Robert Wright
> *The Moral Animal*

The Things That Last

The Talmud says that there are three things that will last: having a child, planting a tree, and writing a book. There's something of substance being communicated in this. But for the sake of exploring this theme, let's assume that you don't want children, don't have a green thumb, and are a terrible writer. What then? We propose that that there are several areas in which we all can participate that lead to a life that lasts. This is by no means exhaustive, but it does move us into the heart of what it means to begin eternal life and extend God's presence in the world. They have the power to change us and become a part of the fabric of who we are. As we approach these things, you'll find that they are very practical. They are things that we can do and practice. Entering into eternal life is not a change in status. It is a change in how we live.

Good...

Have you ever noticed that when you buy a car you suddenly notice all the other cars that are the same model as yours? They've been there all along, but you weren't looking for them. It happens when we buy a new coat, get a dog, or try a new hairstyle. Suddenly we notice all the people who have the same thing.

This same principle holds true in our general disposition in life. If you have a bad attitude and are feeling negative toward the world, then you're going to see all the negative people and events around you. If you have a positive attitude and are looking forward to the day, then you're going to see the good that's around you.

One of us worked in insurance when we were young. Working with claims was an interesting study in human nature. If someone was at fault in an accident, you needed to speak with the person immediately after the accident to get the truth. If more than a few hours had gone by, then the person would be "fuzzy" about who was at fault. If you didn't speak with that same person until the next day, it was never his or her fault.

Paul, an imposing man in his fifties, had an accident with his brand new car. Even before the age of texting, people found other ways to distract themselves while driving, which is exactly what Paul had done. While looking down, he clipped a car parked along the street. Now this may seem an open and shut case, but unfortunately Paul didn't report this until the next day. Obviously by then he wasn't at fault. He had created an elaborate argument about how the car was parked on a slight angle, hence causing the accident. When Paul was sitting in our office and the news was delivered that this would be categorized as his fault, he went ballistic. He had a very colorful vocabulary and he used it all while shouting to everyone within earshot as he stormed out.

After he left, we tried for two weeks to reach Paul, but there was no reply. We suspected that he was lining up a lawyer to advocate for him. Finally, Paul called back. There was no edge to his voice, no hint of anger, just a very calm man apologizing for not calling back sooner. It was then that Paul shared that he had a heart attack shortly after we had last spoken. He was no longer the same man. Suddenly, his car was just a hunk of metal and all he really wanted was to talk about was how "blessed" he was to be alive. And he certainly wasn't using the same colorful vocabulary he had used before! From that day forward, Paul went from a problem client to a person with whom you wanted to speak.

Major life events have a way of refocusing us, but we need not leave the opportunity to change to chance. What if Paul had never had a heart attack? Would he have ever changed? Maybe not. Do we need a brush with death to help us live in a more positive way? Definitely not. There is another way.

There is a verse in Philippians that speaks to this: "Finally, beloved, whatever is true, whatever is honorable, whatever is just, whatever is pure, whatever is pleasing, whatever is commendable, if there is any excellence and if there is anything worthy of praise, think about these things" (4:8). This is more than counsel on how to be a good Christian. It directs us to the path to see the world in a new way.

Just as we notice people who have cars like the one we recently purchased, when we begin to look for what is honorable, just, commendable, and excellent, the world seems full of these things. And the same is true when we look for the things that are awful, wrong, ugly, and poorly done in this world.

A consultant tells of the time he was called in to work with a major accounting firm. Apparently it was a place filled with unhappy workers. What he discovered was that the employees spent eight to fourteen hours a day looking for errors on tax forms, and this molded them into experts at spotting errors.

Unfortunately, this "skill" spilled over into the rest of their lives. The result:

> These accountants experienced each day as a tax audit, always scanning the world for the worst. As you can imagine, this was no picnic, and what's more, it was undermining their relationships at work and at home. In performance reviews, they noticed only the faults of their team members, never the strengths. When they went home to their families, they noticed only the C's on their kids' report cards, never the A's. When they ate at restaurants, they could only notice that the potatoes were underdone—never that the steak was cooked perfectly.[47]

This is not how any of us would choose to live, but without realizing many of us have become experts in scanning the world for what's wrong. Faith calls us to live differently and to look at the world differently. We are to search the world around us for what is true, honorable, just, pure, pleasing, excellent—for anything that is praiseworthy. When we do, we are able to see the beauty of what God has created. The world becomes filled with things that are praiseworthy.

> Everything has beauty, but not everyone sees it.
>
> —Attributed to Confucius

Father Greg, also known as "G" to the homies in his parish in Los Angeles, had Lula pay him a visit one day. Lula was ten years old and struggled in almost every area of his life. On this particular day Father Greg was in a meeting, but Lula was pretty insistent on seeing him. He had a report card in his hand and was beaming, even doing a little dance while he waited. Father Greg was going to make him wait, but knowing that Lula did miserably in school, he had to halt his meeting to see why Lula was so excited to show him his report card. Lula handed Father Greg the card, and he looked at the grades. As his eyes moved down the card he saw F, F, F, F, F, and F! He thought to himself, "All Fs and nothing but damn Fs." He scanned the card to find anything he could praise Lula for, and then finally he saw it: Absences: 0. And so Father Greg said to Lula, "Lula, nice goin', *mijo*, you didn't miss a day." And then he high-fived Lula as he left the office.[48]

It's not always easy, but it's always there. Something good we can acknowledge, something worthy of praise. People who take five minutes each day to contemplate three things that are good and praiseworthy experience a sense of well-being and wholeness that was previously missing. It provides the chance to look over the day and name the "God moments" that were part of their day. In chapter 4 we spoke of looking back on our lives to remember the God moments we've experienced. This is the daily version of this that helps us put Philippians 4:8 into practice. Our praiseworthy moments need not be life-changing, though they could be. It can be getting a parking space close to the entrance, a kiss from your child before she leaves for school, a quiet evening with the one you love, or "Absences: 0" on a report card.

While the advice from Philippians is two thousand years old, researchers are only now learning the significance of doing this. In naming the things that are praiseworthy, several things happen. First, our brains become wired to look for the positive and the possibilities that we can seize. Second, since our brains can only hold so much at one time, when we focus on what's good, we let go of those things that used to frustrate and anger us. Third, focusing on good things creates something that lasts within us. One study found that the people who practice this are happier and less depressed for months, and the impact continues even when people stopped the practice—not that we would advise this.[49] This confirms what people of faith have known for millennia: focusing on what is good and from God creates something that lasts within us.

... and Grateful

Gratitude is another powerful force that creates within us something that lasts. However, gratitude has deteriorated into something that little resembles the gratitude to which faith points us. This can be seen in the growing phenomenon of "humblebrags." Humblebrags are when we express thanks for something, but it is really a way to brag about ourselves. When an eighteen year old tweets, "So thankful to be attending Yale. 31,000 applied, only 1,300 got in," that's a humblebrag. When someone posts on Facebook, "I'm incredibly grateful for the success of my book. Does anyone have tips on handling success?" that's a humblebrag. When someone begins a speech, "I was just honored as a distinguished alum at my university. I'm very appreciative but it does makes me question their standards!" That's a humblebrag.

This is not the essence of gratitude of which faith speaks, nor is it the posture of thankfulness that will change us. Gratitude that is transformational begins with a thankfulness that is directed toward something beyond us. Martin Seligman, a leading researcher on human flourishing, says that gratitude "cannot be directed toward the self."[50] This is why in Ephesians it says to give "thanks to God" (5:20). It doesn't say just to be thankful, but it directs us to God.

It may be helpful to remember that the root of "gratitude" is *gratia*, which means "grace." Grace is the compassion and kindness we experience from God and for which we give God thanks. The posture of gratitude creates a connection with the goodness of God that is infused within creation. It reminds us of what we already have, not what we're lacking. It helps us live and love today, not wait until something is achieved or something is gained. It grounds us in the fullness of life that God offers us each day.

This is not the same as being thankful for everything around us. When we can't pay our bills, when we lose a loved one, or when we are unemployed, we aren't called to thank God for these things. However, we are called to "give thanks in all circumstances" (1 Thess. 5:18). This means that whatever mess we may find ourselves in, we are to look for those things for which we can give thanks. Though we may be unemployed, we can give thanks to God for the people who are helping us find a new job. Though our electricity may have been turned off because of unpaid bills, we can give thanks to God for the family member who let us sleep in his or her home.

> Let us be grateful to the people who make us happy;
> they are the charming gardeners
> who make our souls blossom.
>
> —Attributed to Marcel Proust

The ancients didn't have any clinical evidence to prove that giving thanks to God changed anything. This wisdom was gleaned by observing people. Research now shows that expressing gratitude can be a life-changing practice: "Studies have shown that consistently grateful people are more energetic, emotionally intelligent, forgiving, and less likely to be depressed, anxious, or lonely. And it's not that people are only grateful because they are happier, either; gratitude has proven to be a significant cause of positive outcomes."[51] This last part should not be passed over quickly. We shouldn't wait to express gratitude until we are feeling great. Actually, it is the expression of gratitude that can help us feel better about who we are and where we are in life.

Over time, gratitude changes how we see ourselves and others. But for this to happen it must become a part of the pattern of what we do. We must find ways to express gratitude "at all times" (Eph. 5:20). We encourage you to add giving thanks to your daily practice of naming what's good and praiseworthy in your life. This can be expanded to include others. What would happen if at the end of each day you spent time with your spouse or children talking about things that were praiseworthy and the things for which you're thankful? What would happen if you started your weekly staff meetings by naming three good things from this past week? What if you ended the meetings by mentioning the things and people for whom you're thankful? You and your relationships would never be the same.

Sticks and Stones

As people created in the image of God, we have the potential to be bearers of the divine presence. We may not realize it, but every day holds the possibility of extending God's presence in this world. One of the ways we do this is through the words we use. Too often we give our words short shrift on the potential impact they can make. We think of words more as something we use to communicate and get our point across, not as something that can take on a life of its own and have a lasting impact.

Scripture does not take the use of words lightly. If we go back to Genesis 1, we find that when God spoke, the world came into being. It is through speaking words that the world was created because words hold the power to become a reality that endures. And it is not just God's words, but our words as well. This should cause us all to consider the words we use. By this we're not talking about learning to talk like a Christian and liberally sprinkling our language with "praise the Lord" and "O what a blessing." And it's not about refraining from swearing. It is understanding that our words have the power to bless people and extend the divine presence into one another's lives.

To help us understand this, we can draw upon a biblical metaphor for the impact of our words. In the Epistle of James it says that "the tongue is a fire" and it only takes a small fire to set a forest ablaze (James 3:5–6). This means the impact of our words is the smoke that comes from the fire. Too often we think of our words as steam, especially negative ones. We would like to think that our words, like pure water vapor, will eventually dissipate and disappear. This minimizes the impact of our negative words and doesn't give much potential for our positive ones.

> Sticks and stones may break my bones,
> but words will make me go in a corner and
> cry by myself for hours.
>
> —Attributed to Eric Idle

However, in this metaphor our words are like smoke. Unlike steam, the vapor of smoke also contains gases and soot that will never go away. It can be diluted but it will never fully disappear. The reality is that our words are much more like smoke than steam. Our words become a reality. They become a real force for good or bad, and we can't take them back. When they're malicious and hurtful, they don't go away, though they can be diluted through apologies and forgiveness. And when they are words of blessing and hope, they too don't go away. They become a reality that breathes the divine presence into another person's life.

It's not that we may say one thing that forever changes someone, though it's possible. It is the cumulative effect of the words we use. Every time we say "I love you," "I'm proud of you," or the simple reassurance that "it's going to be ok," we are speaking words of blessing into someone's life. God has given us the ability to speak words that last into one another's lives. If we watch for those moments, God uses our words to breathe the Spirit into someone in a way that will forever shape who they become.

Belonging to a Community That Lasts

In these three examples we have seen how faith opens the possibility of living a life that lasts. There are things that last within us and things that last beyond us. One of the greatest is the community of faith. Within this community we experience true belonging. We walk through the doors and are truly seen for who we are. People see our accomplishments and foibles, yet they welcome us for who we are and where we are in life. This is possible because we are a community bound by God's love and animated by the way of Christ. Our local communities arise from the community that transcends time and place. We are a part of the community that Jesus created. A community that continues to be shaped, nurtured, and passed on by those who have followed since.

We share a spiritual bond with all those who came before us and all those who will come after us. This is known as the communion of saints. This means that when we join the life of a congregation, the spiritual force is greater than the members that are there today. The good that has been done and the love that has been shared by those who passed away long ago still lives within the life of the community. When we celebrate the Eucharist, say the Lord's Prayer, recite the Apostles' Creed, join together in the liturgy, or read from scripture, we are celebrating the spiritual bond we share with those who came before us.

Of course this may sound overly idealistic. Communities of faith, especially local congregations, seemingly succumb to divisions and conflicts that betray the ideals we outline. The spiritual bonds that promise to unite can erode and break under the strain of disputes. Worse, though not widespread, there have been congregational scandals resulting from the misconduct, financial and sexual, of religious leaders. Such instances cast widespread ripples; all leaders and congregations can seem complicit. For some congregations, their wider confessional traditions and institutional affiliations become irretrievably tainted, especially for those persons who have experienced disillusioning behavior firsthand. Fortunately, though the experience is horrific, most people and congregations view it from a distance.

Far more congregations are prone to be venal, riddled with friction, and internally focused. Church members and leaders fret over budgets that fall short and liturgies that fall flat, tiffs between members and sermons that puzzle more than inspire. Congregations can appear far more human than holy, more frail than resolute. Eccentricities and control needs often appear to dominate and faith confession seems more verbally recited than admirably lived.

But it is in just such circumstances that faith takes root. Even the most neurotic and mundane appearances can point beyond themselves to divine presence and faithful possibility. Differences can be mediated and common purpose extended, even amid quirky dynamics. People fully retain their peculiarities and preoccupations. Their opinions and readiness to express them may resist amendment. But they can awaken to a vivid sense of being connected, with those around them and with those who have gone before. Prayer and study and faith tradition generally can animate their lives, and they take pride in sharing what they value. Such awakening is not unusual. It lies at the core of how faith is lived, even in congregations.

As a result, we can affirm that together we share in the high calling of being bearers of the divine presence. We hope we can fulfill this vocation because of the spiritual strength we draw from those who came before us. We say their prayers, we tell their stories, and over time, we create new prayers and new stories for future generations. As we participate in a community of faith, we become a part of the communion of saints. And this is something that lasts!

A Question to Consider As we consider things that last, what are the things that you've done or contributed to that you believe will last?

A Thing You Can Do In chapter 4 we suggested you begin each day with the Serenity Prayer, and now we recommend that you end each day by thinking of three things that happened today for which you're thankful. You can do this alone or make it a part of your family's conversation at the dinner table.

CHAPTER 6

Roll Up Your Sleeves

An Unexpected Gift

Each year, shortly before Christmas, when one of us (William) was a child, the local Episcopal minister would phone and ask if he could stop by for a visit. He had something to deliver, he would hint mysteriously. Expecting the call, the family muttered, "Here it comes." Soon a tall man in a black clergy suit rang the doorbell and a pleasant but predictable visit would begin. The minister never appeared at the family home otherwise. Yet late each year he surfaced.

There would be warm but superficial conversation about the church, the weather, and families. Then he would bring forth a nicely wrapped package and William would be summoned to receive it. There would be effusive expressions of gratitude, even from William once he had been nudged. Being polite to the minister was required, even if we could not decipher his behavior. Each year he turned up and delivered the same innocuous package, apparently in the spirit of the season. Only one element of mystery ever intruded: which bizarre gift would it be this year? There were only two options and he did not always alternate from year to year.

The same gift could appear two years in a row before the other gift returned in the third year.

It was never a joyous prospect, always a puzzling one. If it was the crock of cheese spread laced with port wine, no one in the household liked it. If it was another book about the American Civil War, no one found that topic of interest. Neither gift matched family tastes or interests. The one might rot in the refrigerator; the other could gather dust on a distant shelf. We never knew what to do with the minister's annual gift. Ideally, within days, it would quietly depart, only to be replaced in another year.

Our attitude toward cheese spread and Civil War history could be seen as ungrateful, even snobbish. The minister made an effort and spent money on us. He had taken time, even if he seemed to give the matter little thought. Maybe the gesture made him feel good about himself, one could surmise cynically. Nevertheless, kindness was involved, even if it was misplaced. But the gift was a burden: what to do with it became the issue. Thoughts about who might enjoy it or how it could be conveyed turned to frustration. We had to resolve the minister's dilemma.

> Every gift from a friend is a wish for your happiness.
>
> —Attributed to Richard Bach

What one can do with unwanted gifts can be a challenge. Oddly, the same reaction can surface when gifts that are wanted, even desperately needed, appear on our doorsteps. In "To See and Not See," Oliver Sacks tells the story of a man who dramatically and rather unexpectedly received his sight after forty-five years of blindness. The promised results of eye surgery exceeded expectations. But the gift of sight proved to be an odd, somewhat unwelcome burden. The man's life had been accustomed to blindness; he had learned to make his way in the world as a blind man. With sight his orientation needed readjustment. He could not make sense of the images steadily assaulting him. He could not draw the new range of perceptions coming at him into a concrete sense of wholeness. In effect, the man who had been blind had difficulty receiving the gift of sight. What had promised healing clarity threw his life off stride.[52]

We have described moments of awakening, using the work of Oliver Sacks to do so. We have also depicted the role of such experiences in moving us toward faith. We have used analogies from nature and noted that vision is an apt metaphor for grasping truths that previously have eluded us. We may not have had a single, all-consuming moment of awakening, as we would imagine an ancient saint or a modern medical patient might claim. We may have had small moments of realization that have begun to point in a promising direction. Trust and hope may be more evident and appealing, as the two previous chapters have described. There may even be a sense that an unexpected gift has arrived. So now, what do we do with it? How do we incorporate it into our lives? Will it be used, or will it sit on a remote shelf?

It is frequently said that faith brings "answers" to life's most urgent questions. But as ministers, we know this is not so simple. It would be nice if all ministers needed to do would be to say a few words, make a few gestures, and watch grateful people set off decisively in new and healthy directions. Faith and ministry could be served up regularly like cheese spread to waiting, eager consumers. But faith, life's greatest gift, is not a commodity. It is a way of life. It cannot be ordered and served; it must be cultivated. And no one size fits all. Styles and tastes vary. What works for one person misses the point with another. Each of us must make sense of the gift to which we are awakening. This is the shape of faith as a journey through life.

The idea of a gift lies at the heart of the Christian understanding of faith. For centuries Christians have believed that faith is an assurance of God's love that could neither be earned nor presumed. Rather the assurance that one is loved, and the faith that makes such assurance both possible and lasting, must be accepted as a gift. In theological terms, such a gift is possible because of what is called God's grace. That is, we human beings can only know that we are loved by a radical gift of God, freely given. Grace is God's love seeking to create wholeness and fellowship. But grace must find expression. Our challenge is to accept the gift, to draw it into our lives until it becomes our support and our guide. Love freely given must be freely shared. As the great Protestant theologian Karl Barth suggested, grace is the reason we are able to hope.[53]

> Until we can receive with an open heart,
> we're never really giving with an open heart.
> When we attach judgment to receiving help,
> we knowingly or unknowingly attach judgment to giving help.
>
> —Brené Brown
> *The Gifts of Imperfection:*
> *Let Go of Who You Think You're Supposed to Be*
> *and Embrace Who You Are*

Grace is not simply an abstract category. It is an invitation. Broadly it is the answer to life's questions, which center on personal assurance and hope. We can identify instances of grace as the fruits of some of life's pivotal occurrences. As one example, psychotherapists speak of seeking "breakthroughs" with their clients. Clearly such experiences are moments in which new and powerful insights arise, making sense of life situations that had proven frustrating and unresolved. A breakthrough, comparable to times of religious awakening, can occur suddenly, dramatically, unexpectedly.

Even more than the answer to a specific question or dilemma, a breakthrough opens up new possibilities that had previously been unimagined. More than solving a specific problem, a breakthrough rewrites life's script. It reconfigures one's priorities and one's values. And it points beyond one's life to revise one's relations to others. What had been an obsession or an obstacle in one's life is not simply overcome; it can seem irrelevant in light of one's new paradigm for one's life. Grace is such a breakthrough. It is a realization that continues to unfold and continues to restructure how one lives, and even for what reasons one lives.

Moments of Grace

This is no academic or religious ideal. There must be a way to absorb fresh possibilities awakened by the gift of grace into the human circumstances of our lives. Fortunately there are powerful accounts of people whose lives were dramatically remade by the unexpected gift of God's grace. In some cases, such people already felt themselves to be deeply religious. But they also felt their lives to be lacking and were frustrated by a nagging sense of incompleteness. Still, when it came, grace was unexpected; even more, it led to dramatic reshaping of lives already well defined. The element of surprise is a constant mark of the presence of God's grace.

His first name was Giovanni, though his nickname was Francesco. He was born in 1181 or 1182 to the family of a prosperous merchant in Assisi in the north of Italy. In an age of rivalry and chivalry, he was an energetic youth who once of age volunteered to fight in one of the recurring regional wars. But en route to battle, he had a religious vision that redirected his journey. He returned to Assisi to make sense of his unforeseen experience.

A second and more directive awakening soon followed. On a pilgrimage to Rome he was moved to join a group of poor beggars outside Catholicism's greatest sanctuary, St. Peter's Basilica. As a result he felt moved to live in poverty and to gather followers who would join him. They would model the life of Jesus and lift up respect for all of God's creation. Indeed, this witness has become synonymous with seeing God in all of life. The values of his upbringing were reversed in a sense. Instead of wealth, there was poverty. Instead of competition and conflict there was reverence for all life.

Francesco's band of followers received approval from Pope Innocent III in 1210, though not without objection from papal advisors. Then the group and their founder became known by the name which has become a virtual trademark: the Franciscans. In time, the founder would be known as St. Francis of Assisi and extensive Roman Catholic religious orders bearing the imprint of Francis would follow.[54] Living in religious community dedicated to a life that would follow the model of Jesus, serve the poor, and witness to the sacred qualities of nature, their influence has been profound. Eight hundred years later it is tempting to see the Franciscans, and of course the Roman Catholic Church, as an extensive institution draped in tradition. But its origins must be recalled. A young man named Francesco had an experience and followed it, not only turning around his own life, but reorienting millions of lives ever since.

Part of grace's breakthrough in our lives is the realization that references to God and faith, and even religion, are not sidebars to life's journey. Faith is not simply a membership or an avocation among various other pursuits. Faith becomes the defining category, once we accept the gift of grace. But faith without works is dead, according to the letter of James in the New Testament. By grace through faith, we can discover new possibilities for healthy lifestyles. We can awaken to unforeseen personal freedom and creativity. We can have fresh incentive to join with other people and to serve the world's needs. Simply put, by grace through faith we discover what it means to care. Faithful people are marked by lives of compassion, instinctively giving of themselves in ways that have wide benefit. In a word, the life to which we are invited by the gift of grace through faith is a life of continuing "growth," as we shall now explore.

"Growth" and Connection

On May 24, 1738, in London, England, a man at a crossroads in his career and his personal life returned home after attending a small Bible study group. He had attended the group for some weeks after fleeing the life he had pursued in Savannah, Georgia. Already thirty-five years old, he should have been settled and, given his abilities, advancing in his career. Until that night in 1738, he had worked doggedly but felt he had failed, and events supported that conclusion.

The son of a minister of the Church of England, John Wesley once had been part of a pious student group at Lincoln College, Oxford, what was derisively called a "holt club." Then, once he was ordained in the Church of England, Wesley went to Savannah intent on deepening religious devotion and improving public morality there. His intentions backfired spectacularly. A young woman in whom he had shown modest interest married another man. Apparently indignant, Wesley refused to serve them communion during worship. As public resentment, and talk of legal action, took shape, Wesley quietly escaped back to London. There, somehow, he intended to remake his life.

Instinctively he joined a Bible study group. The pious setting was familiar and scripture promised guidance that now was urgently needed. Once he had been certain of himself and his direction. Now his certainty was limited. But on that May evening, something different occurred. Wesley later recalled that as the Bible was discussed, his "heart was strangely warmed." A new sense of possibility took shape and it lay right in front of him. He began to build a network of small groups for Bible study and he gave them a new twist. The emphasis was on making faith come alive in a person's life. The words on the page could unlock personal challenges to reveal fresh ways of moving ahead in one's life. There could be a living, "vital" faith and one could grasp it.

The possibility unfolded in dramatic ways. First, the network of groups grew extensive, requiring an elaborate organization to manage them. Second, response to Wesley's message and to him personally became so pronounced that not merely groups but whole congregations took shape to carry the message forward. The idea that one could discover a vibrant faith and, just as important, continue to grow in it, drew first thousands, then millions of people. An energetic organizer, Wesley also elicited suspicion from religious and civil authority. But he insisted that a lively faith was also a socially beneficial one. The message was echoed by colleagues, some of whom he had known at Oxford. Their outlooks and intentions varied, but they shared a pursuit of lively personal faith. Wesley's contemporaries included Jonathan Edwards in New England and George Whitefield, whose ministry spanned the Atlantic Ocean. They were the sources of evangelical Christianity. Wesley would become known as the founder of the Methodist Church.[55]

> Faith is to believe what you do not see;
> the reward of this faith is to see what you believe.
>
> —Saint Augustine

Wesley's example extends our understanding of faith. In effect, he posed the question of what happens after an awakening to faith. In other words, what does it mean to "grow" in faith? Like his contemporaries, Wesley had experienced religious awakening. After that powerful time his life began to be different and the result proved historic. Wesley emphasized an ongoing pursuit of "sanctification," or growth in holiness. He dared to advance the idea that the goal of the Christian life was to advance both inwardly and outwardly toward perfect union of one's soul and one's life with God. He would relent only to say that literal perfection was unlikely. But he pressed the necessity of striving for personal perfection as he defined it. The striving mattered, not the literal goal. The effort to draw closer to God and to manifest this closeness in how one lived was what concerned Wesley.

For this reason Wesley, and later Methodism, attached great significance to personal and public morality, as we shall describe later in this chapter. Methodists became known for a distinctive way of life, including abstinence from the consumption of alcoholic beverages and at times public opposition to the sale of alcohol. This was striking because Methodism built great appeal among England's poorest people in industrial areas where alcoholism was rife.

Wesley's awakening to faith was not unprecedented. But after the fires of awakening subsided, he charted a path toward continued growth in faith that centered on life in small groups and deepening personal and social holiness. The imprint of Wesley's method has been lasting. In the twenty-first century the ideals of faith formation and group accountability remain prominent, though their messages may diverge widely from the source and direction of Wesley. The small group setting also has taken on momentum of its own, even apart from religious organizations.

More than Wesley, or his supporters or opponents, could have imagined, we live now in an age of "spiritual independence." That headline loomed over a newspaper article describing how some people in one urban area cultivate the growth in faith Wesley pursued.[56] Detached from "organized religion," as Wesley began outside institutional circles, a number of people cultivate spiritual disciplines, mixing and mingling sources to plot their spiritual journeys. For some literal movement, in the form of yoga or walking a labyrinth, is central. Steps, postures, and pathways become laden with spiritual meaning and help to dramatize one's path toward wholeness and personal realization. Not all such persons invoke "faith," but they speak in congenial terms while relishing pursuit of something like it. The journeys are personal, but crossroads with others occur often. People join to work or discuss or walk or meditate together. They cannot go deeper alone.

Pathways to Growth

Spirituality and spiritual growth come in many forms, reflecting the individualism that characterize them. For example, there is great emphasis now on "mindfulness," a practice with Buddhist roots. Mindfulness entails setting aside time to cultivate focused attention on the present moment, apart from nagging worries about the past or the future. Shedding judgment and intensifying simple awareness, mindfulness is akin to meditation with a theme or idea to offer focus. For some persons, attention to nature weaves throughout mindfulness or helps to guide meditation. Looking outside oneself and living in the moment become central.

Programs in colleges, counseling centers, or independent institutes help to shape these pursuits. They are separate from congregations and traditional forms of worship; they take on more personal timing and focus. Yet classes and talks about spiritual traditions in different religions surface. Themes such as mysticism help to link the personal quest to faith tradition. Another doorway to moving from the immediate and personal to the shared and historic appears. Spiritual growth fosters new links, new ways of linking, and new reasons for being linked.

Though current pathways to spiritual growth seems to bypass the churches, many are attuned and serving throngs of people as a result. Christ Episcopal Church in Charlotte, North Carolina, has grown dramatically since the beginning of the twenty-first century. At that time a large congregation of approximately three thousand members, it has since leaped to nearly six thousand members. Much of this surge is attributable to an emphasis on spiritual growth. Already sponsoring extensive outreach and educational programs, Christ Church has fostered spiritual growth as the necessary basis of its activities. The impact is telling. When a group of lay leaders from the church were interviewed about spiritual growth, their personal independence as well as their commitment to the church and its mission were apparent.

Spiritual growth is a pivotal goal of life in this congregation. Special themes often define program years there. A recent one has been the "Leap of Faith," which encompassed several years. By such themes, Christ Church brings focus and coordination to its many activities. The lay leaders who were interviewed cited "Leap of Faith" as a key reference point. For them spiritual growth entails finding connection to God and to one another that has been awakened by life experiences and shaped by congregational programs. The quality all cited is *connection* as a means to service, knowledge, and a sense of belonging. All point to going deeper in one's faith and one's involvement with others.[57]

> In a futile attempt to erase our past, we deprive the community of our healing gift. If we conceal our wounds out of fear and shame, our inner darkness can neither be illuminated nor become a light for others.
>
> —Brennan Manning
> *Abba's Child: The Cry of the Heart for Intimate Belonging*

The pathways toward spiritual growth vary at Christ Church, but all point in the same direction. Some of those who discussed spiritual growth spoke about finding God in solitude on the church grounds or elsewhere in nature. Some came to the church because of crises that compelled personal change. Several had explicit moments of awakening, construed as spiritual, encouraging them to find grounding in faith community. Others looked back on steady forms of nurture at home and at school as well as in a church. All expressed some surprise at where their lives had gone, including serving as leaders in a congregation. Yet when pressed to explain what spiritual growth meant, who God was, and where their personal lives had gone, all spoke in similar terms.

They all felt led to be in community with other people, in open-ended yet grounded ways. All had come to see their lives as journeys that had steadily blended with one another. For most, their families and even extended families had become close. They viewed life in congenial terms and had built ways of working as well as worshipping together. Some had built considerable track records as volunteers. Above all, they had learned to serve the needs of others, including people outside their congregation.

Service to the poor, hungry, and homeless in Charlotte loomed large for them, and Christ Church maintains significant outreach initiatives as a result. A powerful link between spirituality and service animates this congregation.

It has become commonplace to speak of declining membership in religious institutions, especially in the so-called "mainline" denominations. Indeed, as a matter of sheer numbers, there has been a long-term decline, the Episcopal Church falling by about one-third since its numbers peaked fifty years ago. But several factors must be noted. First, there are readily found instances of congregations of all denominations experiencing numerical growth. Christ Church, Charlotte, is not an isolated instance, though it is an especially dramatic one. Second, numerical growth does not mean today what it did in the mid-twentieth century. Then church vitality was measured by the numbers of members, in individual congregations and in the denominations with which they were affiliated. This was a natural result of the presumed institutional focus of American religion then.

Now, in a diverse and fluid religious environment, with diminished institutional emphasis, membership is less important as a measure of religious life. Instead membership is being replaced by participation. That is, people now intend to find congregations with which they are comfortable, regardless of denominational affiliation, if any. People are drawn to congregations where they find particular programs that appeal, where a dynamic sense of belonging looms. In a growing number of instances, people participate in congregations, perhaps intensely, before they even attend weekly worship services. Becoming a recognized member of the denomination with which a congregation is affiliated is a step that may or may not occur until much later.

This pattern reflects several realities, which we have traced. First, the emphasis on having and exercising personal choice; religious affiliation, much less participation, reflects this priority.

Activity in a congregation can no longer be presumed, and when it occurs its pattern is likely to reflect personal preference at a particular stage of one's life. Second, the affiliation with any congregation now is more likely to reflect an urge to belong for the sake of spiritual growth. Those congregations that thrive are those that actively encourage spiritual growth in ways that do not prescribe but encourage and help to shape a variety of personal journeys.

How does spiritual growth occur? Similarly, what does it mean for faith to develop? The experience of people in Charlotte and in other lively congregations reflects the stages of faith development outlined by James W. Fowler. These stages were formulated a generation ago, but they continue to find resonance with a wide range of spiritual experiences within organized religion as well as beyond it. Fowler depicted faith as "a universal quality of meaning making" formative of a clear, personal "center of value." He perceived a similar course of development across all major faith identities.[58]

Briefly, Fowler's progression begins with an undifferentiated, pre-stage before a scheme of development unfolds in six stages, as follows:

> **Stage 1:** Intuitive-Projective Faith
> Preschool children mix fantasy and reality
> and form basic ideas about God.

> **Stage 2:** Mythic-Literal Faith
> Early school-age children see the world in
> literal, logical ways.

> **Stage 3:** Synthetic-Conventional Faith
> As teenagers, people are inclined to accept
> an all-encompassing belief system and to

hold its authority figures in unquestioning
regard. Many persons remain at this stage.

Stage 4: Individuative-Reflective
In this stage people question assumptions
and authorities and start to take ownership
of their own faith journeys.

Stage 5: Conjunctive Faith
Fowler poses that this stage is difficult
to reach before midlife. Here a person
finds more assurance, reaches personal
"answers," and finds that faith community
has importance. There is also comfort with
different faiths and interest in them.

Stage 6: Universalizing Faith
Few people reach this stage; it is descriptive
of great faith leaders. Life becomes simple,
focused, directed toward basic truths and
service of others. The person can be a role
model for others.

We hesitate about one aspect of Fowler's theory: using major
approaches to human development he aligned his stages with chron-
ological development. We understand that certain approaches to
faith accord with early childhood development, especially the first
several stages. However, faith development now does not always
reflect biological and social development so neatly. Persons who
are older than early childhood may hold literal and logical views
of faith and life, for example. Fowler does note, and we under-
score, that many people remain at stage three, the level of conven-
tional faith and authority figures. However, many people simply
are unformed in faith in any recognizable sense.

Nevertheless we endorse Fowler's trajectory. Faith development and, hence, spiritual growth can be measured in two respects, as he suggests. Both respects represent a person's move from a literal and often rigid state toward, first, connections with other people outside one's family and the locality one has inherited; and, second, service to people in need. In other words, faith development is achieved as one moves outward and acts with specific intention to create wider benefit because of one's maturing faith. In a word, the summation of spiritual growth encompasses participation in community and *compassion*.

Gifts Given as Well as Received

We entitled this chapter "Roll Up Your Sleeves" for several reasons. First, the journey toward faith is hard work, literally the project of a lifetime. Faith is no fixed quality, not a rock to which we cling, nor a clearly marked destination that we either reach or fall short of. As we have noted, in a sense the journey is the destination. As it develops, faith encourages certain qualities of life that sharpen the meaning of our lives and encourage health and wholeness in our lives. The pursuit of such a quality of life proves to be hard work.

Second, the journey of faith that we have described forces us outward, beyond our private feelings and thoughts, away from fixed perceptions and assumptions. Using Fowler's stages of faith development and the example of Christ Church in Charlotte, we can see where the journey of faith points. It revises our priorities and remakes our ways of connecting to other people. It endows us with new ideals of community and even friendship. Lastly it points us toward care for others, not as periodic service projects or charitable donations alone, but as a way of life.

> If you want others to be happy, practice compassion.
> If you want to be happy, practice compassion.
>
> —The Dalai Lama XIV
> *The Art of Happiness*

As a brief sidebar, it is worth noting that faith as a journey is not governed by moral laws or rules imposed by religious institutions. There is no narrow, prescribed faith where one size or style must fit all. Instead faith is a process of discovery, unveiling life-giving patterns of both freedom and responsibility. Religious authorities do not dictate necessary beliefs and behaviors; they could never effectively enforce them. Instead one moves toward both clarity about one's own values and way of life while resting comfortably with those of other people. The beauty of faith, and the wonder of God toward which it points, is the variety of faith quests amid common intention. The details of personal lives and personal faiths may vary, but the pathway has similar direction and reference points. As one advances, one gains from the convictions and experiences of others while being affirmed in one's own confessional identity. God is large enough for all.

The highest quality toward which faith points is *compassion*. Sometimes called "fellow feeling" or loosely identified with "charity," compassion literally means "to suffer with." It represents an active, practical standing with people in the midst of their need. Compassion goes beyond charity as we ordinarily think of it, though there are similarities with the biblical concept of *caritas*. Compassion entails initiative to discover what will actually benefit people and places in need, apart from our impulse to help as we intend. Compassion entails empathy, or feeling with people, more than it involves sympathy, which is feeling for them. Compassionate people do not feel sorry for others, they stay with them in the midst of tough times. Compassion is active and practical, but it is not only about doing. It is the expression of "love of God and love of neighbor" that pervades all the great religions.

For Christians, compassion is cited twelve times in the New Testament. For example, Matthew 9:36 and Mark 6:34 speak of Jesus seeing crowds of people and having compassion for them, apparently because of the extent of their needs. Luke 15 tells the story of the prodigal son who returned home after missteps in his life. Verse 20 of that chapter speaks of the father seeing from afar that his son was returning and feeling compassion for him. Indeed, the son was welcomed home. In these accounts the highest examples of faith arise where one person feels a depth of concern for others and steps forward to care in difficult and painful situations.

The most familiar instance of compassion in the Christian Bible is the parable of the Good Samaritan found in Luke 10:25–37. Parables were a means by which Jesus linked a general truth of faith to particular circumstances that his hearers would recognize. The effect of the parables has been to root Christian faith in how one acts toward others more than what one feels or believes. Doctrines and institutions are secondary; the manner of life in relation to wider worlds is what counts. The familiar story of the Samaritan illustrates what this means. In the story a person from a socially and religiously marginalized people proves to be the one who truly embodies faith's ideal, which is care for people who suffer. The power of the story is obvious; its appeal is timeless. Faith reaches its pinnacle when it prompts engagement with people in need.

But is this only an ideal? Has compassion truly been characteristic of faith traditions or has reality undercut what faithful people intend? Critics of religion frequently allege that claims of compassion are contradicted by reference to history. Indeed, the historical legacy is complex. But on balance the instances of compassion outweigh the failings of religious people. Compassion has become religion's hallmark. Long-lasting social benefit has been the result.

We have explained that John Wesley developed an elaborate view of the pursuit of "sanctification," or personal growth in holiness. The idea was more than a defining theological category as the Methodist movement arose. Methodists became noted for advocacy of social reform, and not merely opposition to the consumption of alcoholic beverages. Methodists became advocates of prison reform and among England's earliest opponents of slavery. In England and America, measures of relief for poor people and eventual emphasis on improving industrial working conditions became key Methodist planks. At the same time, Methodism in the United States founded educational institutions that now rank among the nation's finest, including Duke, Emory, and Northwestern universities.

Nor is Methodism alone. Every major branch of Christianity can be cited for founding hospitals and clinics, schools and colleges. Advocacy of human rights and embrace of suffering people also are integral. The impulse extends to congregations where feeding programs, tutoring, job training, homeless shelters, support for battered women, counseling centers, and more are found. Often clusters of congregations jointly sponsor programs that one or two would find difficult to sustain. In Richmond, Virginia, for example, dozens of congregations representing various faiths have collaborated for several decades to provide shelter, meals, and job prospects for homeless persons. Their acronym, CARITAS, stands for Churches Around Richmond Involved To Assure Shelter; it is derived from the Latin word for charity. The otherwise awkward title conveys an ideal of faith that underscores our point. Compassion, closely tied to the biblical notion of charity, is an ideal people of faith prize. Ceaselessly they strive to make it real.

> Until he extends the circle of his compassion
> to all living things,
> man will not himself find peace.
>
> —Albert Schweitzer

What has prompted this ideal and the hard work its pursuit demands? Few lives in the history of Christianity witness more dramatically to compassion, and the faith that drives it, than the life of Albert Schweitzer. Born in Germany in 1875, he died in Africa, his adopted home, in 1965. Schweitzer was a polymath, an accomplished musician and a well-published theologian. He left a lasting imprint on academic analysis of the life of Jesus, especially consideration of how facts and myths about his life intermingled. His impact was felt early in life; one of his most important books appeared when he was thirty-one.

But by the age of thirty he had resolved to become a medical missionary. His calling required medical education. By the age of thirty-eight, he had completed training, married, found a sponsoring organization, and raised money to start a small hospital. He promptly went to Gabon, on the west coast of Africa, where he would spend most of the rest of his life. When asked why, he had a simple explanation: he wished to follow the example of Jesus. He had a reverence for life and regard for human dignity that arose from faith. To be a person of faith was to serve with little regard for one's own comfort or benefit. Instead, pursuit of healing and the common good defined his life.[59]

Schweitzer's achievements were exemplary. But his faith and its expression were not unusual. One weekday morning a church's monthly breakfast program featured a panel of men reflecting on faith as they neared retirement. All three of them cited turning points in their lives. One had a near brush with death as a young adult. Another had lost an adult son to heart disease after lengthy hospitalizations. All could speak of loss, in terms of loved ones dying or projects not panning out. All hinted at family ties as well as family tensions.

But in each case they spoke emphatically of growth in faith and newfound impulses to benefit the lives of other people as well as the community in which they live. "I found a new vocation," one man over seventy declared. "I want to be there for people in their struggles." Then he added, "This has become a beautiful thing. I have something to give back because of what I have been through." Healing from the loss of his son, he felt he had received a gift. So he resolved to give as well as to receive.

A Question to Consider What understanding of spirituality did you have before reading this book, and how would you define spirituality today?

A Thing You Can Do Many people engage in acts of kindness and compassion but don't use it as an opportunity to grow in faith. The next time you extend compassion to another person, reflect on its meaning for your journey of faith and what it teaches you about things that have significance in life.

Conclusion

The Inescapable Questions of Faith

Many people can recall when the questions first surfaced forcefully for them. They can tell you where they were and what they were doing. Details like how hot it was and whether or not it was raining are recalled clearly. Sometimes they were in the midst of a large, public event, which others would also recall. We can't entirely walk through life, or face its transitions, alone, in the privacy of our thoughts. Even when the questions surface deep within us, they soon pop to the surface of our lives. We may try to isolate our vulnerable selves, but other people soon notice; something is going on within us.

It doesn't have to happen suddenly as if by spontaneous combustion. Often the questions simmer within us, and we barely notice. Eventually they are triggered, at times by something slight, at times by personal crisis, or by events in the public arena. However it happens, the questions come roaring at us and soon frame all of life. We can see little else. Before then, we were able to evade by elaborate denial. But the bubble of denial eventually bursts and the questions are before us: who are we and what do we believe? They are the questions of faith.

Television journalist David Gregory heard the questions from an unlikely source: the then president George W. Bush asked Gregory unexpectedly, "How's your faith?" Over time the presidential inquiry sent Gregory on a search dedicated to making sense of his fragmented life. There was no overt sign of crisis, but he awakened to a nagging lack of clarity. His family background was mostly Jewish and somewhat Catholic. His wife was devoutly Protestant. But far more than institutional affiliation was at stake. As he explored, more questions appeared.[60]

Faith runs deeper than institutions, affiliations, and traditions, though it is incomplete without them. Faith is rooted in who we are as individuals, each one of us in transit, somewhere along life's journey. The questions of faith soon multiply. Who are you and what do you believe? Where is your life headed and how do you propose to get there? These are the inescapable questions that arise, sooner or later in our lives. At some point, with force or with subtlety, we face these questions and still others that emerge from them.

> Did I offer peace today? Did I bring a smile to someone's face? Did I say words of healing? Did I let go of my anger and resentment? Did I forgive? Did I love? These are the real questions. I must trust that the little bit of love that I sow now will bear many fruits, here in this world and the life to come.
>
> —Attributed to Henri Nouwen

We are defined by how we respond to these core questions in the midst of circumstances we likely did not choose and would prefer to avoid. Some of these moments may be challenging and stressful, even threatening, but often we know what to do. If there is a fire, we call the fire department. If we witness, or are caught up in, an automobile accident, we call the police and emergency medical assistance if needed. Such times may test our readiness to respond, but may not probe the depths of our faith. What we believe and who we may be likely are irrelevant and distracting questions at times when we must act quickly. What is needed from us at such times usually is apparent.

But many times of life crisis are unclear. Many decision moments do not pose clear choices. Ministers repeatedly meet with people facing situations they struggle to comprehend, trying to sort out what they believe in the process. Often they see no appealing options and feel trapped and powerless. Yet they must do something. In some cases, a loved one is in intensive care on a respirator with little promise of recovery. The family has an advanced medical directive but can they really agree to end treatment and prompt death? How can they decide? They must ask: who we are and what do we believe?

At other times, a spouse or partner behaves erratically on a regular basis, increasingly in public. There are mood swings, broken promises, and unattended responsibilities. Is there drug or alcohol abuse? Is an underlying emotional weakness being triggered? The downward spiral advances without interruption. Ordinary kindness and patience are brushed aside, and the relationship frays. What can the worried spouse, and perhaps a wider family, do? What are their options? Who are they, and what do they believe, about relationships and commitments and family ties? Such questions surface intensely.

A woman's chemotherapy proves less effective than hoped; the side effects intensify and the benefits diminish. What should she do? Across town, a young man's arrival in college proves less than enthralling. He is depressed and his parents are worried. Worse, the parents are separating and communication between them has broken down, even about their son's plight. On a nearby street a woman who is single with a young child cannot sleep. She has an uneasy feeling about the accounting practices of the company where she works. Hints of illegal activity cross her e-mail list. What should she do? She is the sole provider for her child and this job arrived after a long period of unemployment. What does she believe; what will her actions reveal about who she is?

In this book we have challenged two notions of faith: first, that faith is simple, fixed, and unchanging. Instead we have depicted faith as a journey, along which we are drawn toward deeper, more grounded and genuine qualities of life that transform who we are. More than moral law or religious affiliation, faith is both the pathway we walk and the way we walk it.

Second, we have challenged the idea that faith gives us "answers" that arise from religious dogma. Instead faith is rooted in questions whose pursuit illumines obscure parts of the world and our own inner recesses as well. In that sense faith is a beacon calling us to move ahead and guiding us in our unsure, tentative steps. The pursuit of faith is a cultivated art or skill, like learning to sculpt or paint, like learning to swim or type. As we practice, the motions become more natural, and we make them our own. Like any art, we never perfect it. But we grow into it and make its cultivation the cornerstone of who we are.

The Art of Faith

How do we do this? For centuries people have asked questions of faith, and for centuries paths toward growth in faith have proliferated, in every religion. That some of these ways of measuring faith development have lasted attests to their truth. For example, Ignatius Loyola (died 1556) was the founder of the Society of Jesus, or Jesuits, one of the influential religious orders of the Roman Catholic Church. Loyola stamped the Jesuits with his "Spiritual Exercises" as a basis for spiritual growth as well as a means of training aspirants to the order. The Exercises serve as a means to discern one's relationship to God and to encourage one to deepen that relationship. The spiritual self-review is a pivotal component and has been applied broadly. One could follow the Exercises on retreat for an intended month, but one could also follow them outside a monastic setting under the guidance of a spiritual director.[61]

Inherent in the Exercises is the opportunity to grapple with how one is doing in one's spiritual life. A broad, general approach allows for individual experience and personal application. But the pathway points in the same direction and takes a common course. The goal is to deepen one's relationship to God through personal commitment to Jesus. Five centuries of Ignatian spirituality now confirm the worth of this approach. Of course it is only one approach; there are innumerable religious and spiritual approaches and measures of personal growth. Finding one that fits your own experience is part of the journey. It may be reassuring to know that people for centuries have sought a scheme of personal growth. It may be disheartening to realize that the variety of approaches, with no obvious way to sort through them, is part of our fragmentation. How can we decipher how we are doing and how can we stay on course?

The questions are not easily answered. By contrast, if you're driving on a highway you can gauge how many miles remain to your destination. If you've never been there, a GPS can guide you to the exact spot. But there is little analogy for the journey of faith. The destination is not so readily defined, the distance to it is unclear, and the route is uncertain. One thing is clear: the pathway of faith zigs and zags; few stretches are straight and well-marked. Deciphering where one is, how one is doing, and where one is headed become all-consuming questions. They echo relentlessly as you try to sort yourself out. You can't avoid asking the questions of faith, at some point or other in your life. When you do, the questions multiply without immediate clarity, much less firm answers. At times the answers even seem beyond reach.

It becomes tempting to foreclose the journey; the questions become overwhelming, the ambiguity incessant and oppressive. We prefer certainty to the cloud of unknowing. It is no wonder that, as a result, fundamentalist religious systems pose promising but ultimately false assurance. The journey of faith cannot be about who is saved or lost, who is morally acceptable versus who must be morally shunned and condemned. The need for personal and collective certainty can prompt horrific forms of exclusion and prejudice. Even violence in the name of sacred truth can appear. The readiness of some to ostracize, and even abuse, others in the name of absolute truth is an abuse of the divine toward which faith points. Religious ideals are open to personal appropriation, but such flexibility in the great religions makes them susceptible to extreme interpretations and applications.

This danger arises because none of us rests comfortably with ambiguity in our lives. We want answers to life's pressing questions, just as we are impatient with obstacles in daily life. At some level we grasp that our lives are fragmented, parceled out among various circumstances and relations and challenges. Some days we are on the verge of making some sense out of things, then more texts and tweets deflect us and further complicate our lives. Small wonder that many of us crave simple, well-packaged answers. But so many supposed answers and gurus urging them fail us. We are left to take literal and symbolic journeys we never imagined. When it is almost too much, insights and discoveries surface. There are answers to the faith questions we ask just around life's next corner.

> Not all those who wander are lost.
>
> —J. R. R. Tolkien
> *The Lord of the Rings*

In this book we have pushed toward answers: we have described the contours of faith, with emphasis on seeking a meeting ground of what people experience and ask, and what faith traditions, especially Christianity, affirms. Our faith convictions and our experience as clergy have shaped our narrative. We have resisted religious simplicity and rigidity, because we see breadth and charity in Christianity. We view the questions that arise on the faith journey as inescapable. So, then, is it possible to measure the journey of faith? How can we know where we are? In general, we conclude, faith concerns sacred reality and what we build on its basis.

Toward Sacred Presence

In his last book, *Convictions: How I Learned What Matters Most*, the late Marcus Borg outlined his own journey in faith. There was a religious background, in the Lutheran Church, set in the American Midwest. But then there were intellectual, political, and religious awakenings, as we have termed them. Because of those things an inherited notion of God was challenged. The idea of the sacred that had been inherited gradually was discarded, and the way it was dispersed resonates beyond Borg's own life and circumstances. More than rejecting what he once believed, Borg awakened to a new depth of reality, and a new framework for faith. His experience as well as his writing make for instructive reading.

Like many, Borg's childhood years bequeathed an image of God as supernatural and yet directing nature and human events along moralistic lines. Notions of reward and punishment structured the view of God, but little reward seemed imminent. Only a narrow doorway to salvation in a next life beckoned. Through it only believers in Jesus of the proper sort would pass. All others would be lost. Details of this view can vary, though various strands of Christian experience have presumed it, as Borg once did. But by the second half of the twentieth century this view had begun to fracture. It is a view and an experience of God that has not disappeared; clearly it is intact in fundamentalist circles. But for many more people it has proven untenable. If God is, then God must be different than such habitual images. By a means he hardly expected, Borg discovered a very different God.

By his own definition, Borg on occasion had brief "mystical" experiences. For just a moment or two the world would suddenly be bathed in light. He would experience an all-encompassing wonder and delight. He would focus not on distinctions between objects and people, but on their unity. He would discover connections, especially between himself and all that was around him. The experience would pass as abruptly as it arose. But Borg carried from it a new sense of seeing and knowing, which he would consider and relish. The feeling of being left with new and valuable perspective and insight strikes us as akin to the sorts of awakenings we have detailed in this book. The fact that Borg felt connected to nature as well as to other people echoes the importance of the human place in larger worlds. Nature is often the setting and the substance of the awakenings to faith we have described.

Then Borg experienced a longer, more intense encounter with wonder and light. On a flight from Tel Aviv to New York the experience appeared and lasted for upwards of forty minutes. The ordinary features of an airplane cabin and its passengers were joined in an aura of beauty. Again there was the feeling of seeing beneath life's surface, and of knowing in ways that transcend daily awareness. Borg, of course, brought to this moment the acumen of a scholar of religion. He could turn to Rudolph Otto's description of the holy as "numinous." He could compare his own moments with William James's analysis of mysticism. He also was struck by Martin Buber's depiction of the experience of God as an "I-Thou" relationship, a profound sense of personal presence beyond judgment and daunting moral standards. Borg's intellectual tools brought assurance that his experience was not unprecedented nor somehow amiss.[62]

He was in good company. Not only scholars of the past several centuries, but the biblical record itself, speak of divine presence in ways strikingly contemporary. The calling of Paul to be a follower of Jesus, recorded in Acts 9:1–19, describes overwhelming light enveloping Saul, as he was then known, as he walked along the Damascus road. A voice, identifying itself as Jesus, challenged him to go to the city and await instructions, which he did. The transition to being a follower had just begun, and he was still known as Saul. For three days he was without sight, until a man named Ananias prayed with him. Then his vision returned and his new life began.

The experience of God is replete with questions, hesitations, and even doubts. The Hebrew Bible records the story of the calling of the prophet Samuel, in 1 Samuel 3:1–10. As a boy, Samuel assisted an elderly prophet named Eli. In the middle of the night young Samuel repeatedly heard a voice calling him and he rushed to Eli, who replied that he did not call. At last Samuel and Eli grasped that the call was divine, and pointed toward a vocation as a religious leader. The passage concludes with Samuel simply saying, "Speak, for your servant is listening."

Despite thousands of years of such accounts, there have also been recurring denials that such experiences could have any factual basis; i.e., that God exists. The writings of Sam Harris and

Richard Dawkins, Christopher Hitchens, and Daniel Dennett represent readings of human and natural processes that preclude any nonmaterial, "divine" reality. Even so, the conclusions of these and other contemporary atheists are contested by stubborn, historic patterns of experience for which their accounts seem inadequate.[63] The whole of human experience consistently seems greater than the sum of its parts. We are more than biological, and especially neurochemical, processes. But some of the atheist arguments, which we do not have opportunity to elaborate here, confuse human biology with philosophical debates with expressions of religious intention in churches and other institutions. Atheists argue that religion is untrue because God or divine reality does not exist, and that religion is untrue because institutions misrepresent its ideals.

There is another strand of writing no more receptive to experience of the divine, but intent on rescuing Christianity, and other religions, from God. Daniel Maguire, a former Roman Catholic priest and theologian in a Catholic university, apparently has finished with God, and is nearly done with the church. Instead he wants to rescue Christianity as a set of ethical principles from the baggage of doctrine and authority. Similarly, the last book of the noted legal scholar Ronald Dworkin wanted to chart a way to have religion without God. Like Maguire, Dworkin focused on Christianity, and other religions, as necessary sets of ethical principles and ideals of human community to be extracted from outmoded images of the sacred.[64]

Christianity's goal is not escape from this world.
It loves this world and seeks to change it for the better.

—Marcus Borg
*Speaking Christian: Why Christian Words Have Lost Their
Meaning and Power and How They Can Be Restored*

Such appeals, and the assertions of atheists who want none of any of it, touch emotional nerves in people. The entanglement of experience of the sacred, with older images of God and with the machinations of religious institutions, is profound. Some people will never disentangle them. To speak of sacred presence is to conjure indelible organizational and authoritarian images. As a result, the sacred is irretrievably laden with judgment, demand, and moralism. The issue is not easily resolved. It is tempting to imagine that core ideals of faith, such as love of God and love of neighbor, can be rescued from religious dogmas and rigid religious institutions. The broad appeal of "spirituality" and "spiritual" community attests to both the unpopularity of "religion" and the longing for faith. But such a distinction is unrealistic, even naïve. Such a stark distinction cannot be lived, much less balanced somehow in one's mind. To be real, faith must be lived, grounded in both human experience and social forms. Faith must be framed by religious tradition which informs and guides it, and channeled by organization which intends to express it in vital forms.

Marcus Borg is one example of an effort to address the tension between the religious "baggage" of the past and the religious yearnings of the present. He has worked to retrieve Christian notions of God, with what we view as fruitful results. For him, as a biblical scholar, ancient texts and traditions attest to experience of a reality that opens up wonder, creativity, encouragement, as well as challenge. God's presence erupts as inspiration and companionship, invitation and guidance. Above all, tapping Buber and Jewish insights, Borg explains that the core of the Christian faith entails being connected to a reality beyond ourselves that is present in all of our lives. He speaks of "panentheism," or of all reality being immersed in divine reality. Everything is in God, and we see this when we awaken to wonder and purpose and, above all, connection: that is, connection to one another predicated on a feeling of being linked beyond and yet within immediate, even material reality. On the basis of connection, we must build a better way with one another. This is faith's core task.

What We Can Build

Our description of faith and the sacred presence to which it points is nearly complete. We have defined faith in terms of basic qualities of life such as trust and hope that can arise in the circumstances of our lives. We have also traced faith to what such circumstances may require of us, including choices that compel attention to personal values and priorities. Faith is rarely a calm decision enacted once and then secured. It often begins as an interruption, usually unwelcome, that moves to a novel sense of presence, and then connection, beyond one's familiar boundaries. But the essence of faith, as we have emphasized, lies in making choices that lead to a life of significance. We learn to make choices as we might learn an art form. Our ways of making choices, even crucial ones, is never perfected. But we can develop skills that enhance how and what we choose while being attuned to our connection to a reality and a power that transcends our ordinary instincts.

Faith is then a journey whose meaning unfolds as it proceeds. Consistently the journey points outward toward connections with other people and the wider world that are both revitalized and novel. Like the journey of faith itself, these connections must be built and even then cannot be presumed. Like a garden of germinating plants and flowers, the connections faith prompts must be tended. Inevitably they will shift, rising and falling. Through them the meaning of faith, and the very meaning of our lives, can deepen. In effect this is the meaning of "growth."

References to "growth" are almost as frequent as references to spirituality itself today. It is notable that "spiritual growth" has become a common though vaguely defined ideal. As a sidebar it is notable that "growth" is not consistently viewed in religious terms. In fact, the two references, growth and religion, seem incompatible. Where growth conveys dynamism and personal meaning, religion suggests rigid authority that glosses over personal priorities and journeys. Yet one's journey toward faith defies popular images of religion; it involves movement toward connection and the possibilities of what can be built as a result. This movement and the question of what can be built is not being asked for the first time. The history of religious life, in particular Christianity, reveals repeated instances of attention to the questions we ask now. Because of faith, what can we build together and how? In the earliest Christian experience what could be built was the principal concern.

Once upon a time the Christian faith was not a religion in the sense that is familiar now. In its beginnings Christianity was a movement. There were no institutions, no hierarchies, no doctrines. In ways that still require explanation, people of various social classes began to gather to talk about their experience of a man named Jesus. At first there were no written accounts of him, though that changed quickly. As we can now see there was both similarity and variation in these accounts and in the lives of early Christian communities. But on major points of faith and practice consensus emerged. Soon literature about the early Christian communities also emerged, recording their activities and helping to deepen their faith.

Early Christianity stretched from Palestine around the Mediterranean, growing vigorously westward. Christianity's growth followed the sea lanes and trade of two thousand years ago. The first Christians included merchants and traders. But though they revealed similar patterns of growth, the first Christian communities were not well connected. In each city around the Roman world there were small gatherings struggling to make sense of the improbable experience of faith they shared. How to understand and build on this experience absorbed their common life.

There was informality in the early Christian gatherings. They met as Jesus and his apostles met for a meal, for prayer, for discussion. Gradually they organized, especially around worship, teaching, and acts of charity. They cared for poor and ill persons who shared the faith; but the scope of compassion grew as they became organized and amassed resources. The fifth chapter of the Letter of James illustrates this point:

> Are any among you suffering? They should pray. Are any cheerful? They should sing songs of praise. Are any among you sick? They should call for the elders of the church and have them pray over them, anointing them with oil in the name of the Lord. The prayer of faith will save the sick, and the Lord will raise them up; and anyone who has committed sins will be forgiven. Therefore confess your sins to one another, and pray for one another, so that you may be healed. The prayer of the righteous is powerful and effective.
>
> vv. 13–16

The idea that the Christian community was a special fellowship called a "church" reflected the intention they shared. The earliest generations of Christians did not envision that they were creating an institution as the term is understood today. They were securing the gift of faith, clarifying its implications, and broadly offering the love it embodied. Religious institutions came later, as complexity and variation in the Christian life demanded clarity and organization.

Yet Christians never have been of one mind. Nor have Christians lost touch with their humanity, for both good and ill. Stunning acts of care and devotion surface throughout the history of the movement that became a religion. But recurring forms of laxity and shortcoming have compelled efforts to reclaim the wonder of the early Christian years, when faith outshone excesses and compromises that crept in. Returns to small groups, to basic questions of faith, and to core purpose together have happened repeatedly. The historic figures we have cited, such as John Wesley, represent such attempts. And there is a similar impulse now.

In such times, personal experiences blend and common ground appears as people meet to discuss what has happened to them. In such gatherings people who have been lonely and even desperate discover that others have faced painful times and asked similar questions. Finding personal answers and direction overwhelms personal capabilities, though the stubborn urge to plunge ahead is not easily overcome. With companions, the journey becomes manageable, often joyfully so. The possibilities for what can be accomplished because of shared faith are limitless.

Although it is tempting to imagine that ancient Christianity pervaded the Roman world and proved homogeneous, this was hardly the case. Even at the time of their legal recognition in 313 CE, Christians may have numbered little more than 10 percent of the Roman population. The influence they amassed centered on their capacity to shape lives in ways that created broad benefit. Christianity arose in a world that was fragmented and uncertain. Avid efforts to answer life's inescapable questions prompted the rise of cults and cult figures, philosophies and rituals. Our world today has changed little in that regard. The search for faith is timeless. The spiritual impulse is innate. The rise of faith community, and even religion on its basis, is inevitable.

The point is being made not only by religious leaders and theologians. A psychologist, Lisa Miller, has located spirituality as a crucial factor in human development, from childhood onward. Her recent book, *The Spiritual Child*, offers scientific footing for the spiritual instinct and for the questions that it encourages.[65] Far from a luxury or a debatable reality, spirituality is pivotal for personal well-being. At first blush this cannot be equated with religion; Miller herself hesitates to take such a step. But the spiritual nature that she outlines points directly toward faith as we have described. If spirituality raises dimensions of human experience that must be addressed, faith is the journey and the destination that result. In turn, religion—as community and as shared purpose—follows naturally. How can spiritual development occur, beyond the orbit of parents and wider family? How can the grounding of one's faith journey happen apart from lessons learned in faith community?

> The possibility of an experience of Christian spirituality for even non-Christian seekers lies precisely in the humanity of Jesus and his ability to be approached and understood by any other human being.
>
> —Roger Haight
> *Christian Spirituality for Seekers:*
> *Reflections of the Spiritual Exercises of Ignatius Loyola*

Such tasks are the historic role of religious congregations. They offer the necessary shift from personal quest to shared purpose. Faith, we conclude, must point us as individuals toward wider worlds, leading us ever outward, by the force of choices we make. Faith includes the movement toward common ground with others, and toward compassion for all in need. Faith centers on connections we cultivate to that which is dynamically true and worthwhile. Faith awakens perspective, on others, and on the long legacy of human journeys toward commitment and community. Because we have been touched by sacred presence, we must never look back, nor remain still. The journey is never concluded. Its continuation enhances us further. Spirituality and religion meet under the umbrella of faith. There, life beyond our imagining becomes possible.

Final Questions to Consider

- Faith and spirituality are about our connection to others. God lives in us when we love others (1 John 4:12). Think of those close to you—your family, friends, and colleagues. Gradually shift your focus from worries and criticisms to ask a single question: what are these key people like when they are at their best? What do you see when you look at them through the lens of God's love? What do you gain by your attachment to them?

- If faith involves choices and large decisions, what are the major decisions that are before you? How will you draw upon your faith and community of faith to help you make decisions that lead to a life of significance?

- One final question: faith often entails risks, though not usually the risk of physical harm. What risks do you fear as your journey of faith deepens? What might you have to give up and who might be affected? What will you have to do differently, and thus make you seem different to the people around you? For what must you stand up and speak out, where previously you may have kept silent?

Things You Can Do to Continue the Journey of Faith

- We have seen that faith is a progression, a journey, outward and yet ever inward. One thing you can do is to keep a journal or diary, charting your journey. Pay special attention not only to the moments when you sense God, but also to the interruptions in your life and what they might communicate. Many, perhaps most, will be mundane. But when you look beneath the surface, what values and perceptions guide your response to the things that disturb the flow of your faith? Faith requires listening and watching.

- To guide your disciplined reflections and self-analysis, you should consider enlisting the services of a trained spiritual director. This need not be the same as therapy or counseling. A spiritual director would not help you to resolve issues, but to see their deeper meaning in terms of the journey of faith.

- In addition to asking yourself such questions as these, and the others at the end of each chapter, you should consider tangible steps that lead you outward, beyond sole focus upon yourself. These could include:

  » Joining a prayer or study group;

  » Giving regular time commitment to programs that feed hungry people or assist the homeless;

  » Becoming involved with the worship life of a congregation, including participating in worship or helping to set up for worship;

» Going on retreat at a monastery or retreat center,
   especially under the guidance of trained and
   skilled retreat leaders;

» Seeking to deepen or create friendships and joint
   projects with persons of other faiths. The projects
   might include working to benefit people in need or
   to serve your local community.

Notes

1 Brené Brown, *I Thought It Was Just Me (but It Isn't): Making the Journey from "What Will People Think?" to "I Am Enough"* (New York: Avery, 2007).

2 James Davison Hunter, *To Change the World: The Irony, Tragedy, and Possibility of Christianity in the Late Modern World*, Kindle edition (Oxford: Oxford University Press, 2010), 209.

3 James Fowler, *Stages of Faith: The Psychology of Human Development and the Quest for Meaning* (New York: HarperCollins, 1995), 5.

4 Augustine, *The Confessions*, Book X, Chapter 8, trans. Henry Chadwick (Oxford: Oxford University Press: 2009).

5 Eleni Towns, "The 9/11 Generation: How 9/11 Shaped the Millennial Generation," *Center for American Progress* (September 8, 2011), https://www.americanprogress.org/issues/religion/news/2011/09/08/10363/the-911-generation/.

6 These generational differences are known as "life cycle effects, period effects and cohort effects." See the Pew Research Center, "Millennials: Confident. Connected. Open

to Change" (February 24, 2010), http://www.pewsocialtrends.
org/2010/02/24/millennials-confident-connected-open-to-
change/.

7 Adapted from Michael T. Robinson, "The Generations:
What Generation Are You?" http://www.careerplanner.com
/Career-Articles/Generations.cfm.

8 Pew Research Center, "America's Changing Religious
Landscape" (May 12, 2015), http://www.pewforum.
org/2015/05/12/americas-changing-religious-landscape/.

9 Hunter, 206.

10 Barry Schwartz, *The Paradox of Choice: Why More is Less*
(New York: Harper Perennial, 2005), 9.

11 "Event Transcript: Religion Trends in the U.S." (August
19, 2013), http://www.pewforum.org/2013/08/19/event-
transcript-religion-trends-in-the-u-s/.

12 Amy Sullivan, "Church Shopping: Why Americans
Change Faiths," *Time* (April 28, 2009), http://content.time.
com/time/nation/article/0,8599,1894361,00.html.

13 Alison Fields and Robert Kominski, "America: A
Nation on the Move," *United States Census Bureau* (December 10,
2012), http://blogs.census.gov/2012/12/10/america-a-nation-
on-the-move/.

14 Lucy Bregman, *The Ecology of Spirituality: Meanings,
Virtues, and Practices in a Post-Religious Age*, Kindle edition (Waco,
TX: Baylor University Press, 2014), Kindle location 299.

15 Martin Seligman, *Flourish: A Visionary New Understanding
of Happiness and Well-Being*, Kindle edition (New York: Free
Press, 2011), Kindle location 4103.

16 Jonathan Haidt, *The Happiness Hypothesis: Finding Modern
Truth in Ancient Wisdom*, Kindle edition (New York: Basic Books,
2006), 88.

17 Ibid., 192.

18 Commentary on Matthew 22:37–38 in *The New Interpreters Study Bible,* Walter J. Harrelson, ed. (Nashville: Abingdon Press, 2003), italics added.

19 *The Journals of Lewis and Clark* (New York: Mariner Books, 1997), entry for June 3, 1805.

20 Noted at various online sites, such as *The Paul Mercurio Show* (March 2015), and at *www.haydenplanetarium.org.*

21 Sebastian Junger, *The Perfect Storm* (New York: W. W. Norton & Company, Inc., 1997).

22 Henry David Thoreau, *Walden* (York: Empire Books, 2013).

23 Becca Kahn, "Photographic Memory," in "Shake Your Tree." Cited in the *Nassau Weekly* (October 17, 2015), *www.nassauweekly.com.*

24 On Nicholas and his vision, see Mircea Eliade, *The History of Religious Ideas, Volume 3: From Muhammad to the Age of Reforms,* trans. Alf Hiltebeitel (Chicago: University of Chicago, 1988), 211.

25 William A. Christian Jr., *Visionaries: The Spanish Republic and the Reign of Christ* (Oakland: University of California Press, 1996).

26 See Ann Taves, *Fits, Trances and Visions: Experiencing Religion and Explaining Experience from Wesley to James* (Princeton: Princeton University Press, 1999).

27 Augustine, *The Confessions.*

28 T. S. Eliot, *Collected Poems, 1909–1962* (San Diego: Harcourt Brace Jovanovich, 1991).

29 David Brooks, "The Subtle Sensations of Faith," *New York Times* (December 22, 2014).

30 Oliver Sacks, *Hallucinations* (New York: Vintage, 2013).

31 Ibid., 293.

32   See Jonathan Aitken, *John Newton: From Disgrace to Amazing Grace* (Wheaton: Crossway, 2013).

33   Allison Seay, parishioner at St. Stephen's Episcopal Church, Richmond, VA, from a reflection at a contemporary service in 2015.

34   Walter Kirn, *Up in the Air* (New York: Anchor, 2002).

35   Cheryl Strayed, *Wild: From Lost to Found on the Pacific Coast Trail* (New York: Vintage, 2013).

36   Robert Southey, *Common-place Book.* 1850 (London: Forgotten Books, 2015).

37   Elisabeth Kubler-Ross, *On Death and Dying: What the Dying Have to Teach Doctors, Nurses, Clergy and Their Own Families* (New York: Scribner, 2014).

38   See Roger Scruton, *The Soul of the World* (Princeton: Princeton University Press, 2014). Also, his Gifford Lectures published as *The Face of God: The Gifford Lectures* (New York: Bloomsbury Academic, 2012).

39   Brian McLaren, "A Reading of John 14:6," *http://www.brianmclaren.net/emc/archives/McLaren%20-%20John%2014.6.pdf.*

40   Eugene H. Peterson discusses this difference based on his reading of Barth, in *The Pastor: A Memoir*, Kindle edition (New York: HarperOne, 2011), 90.

41   Commentary on John 6:27 in *The New Interpreters Study Bible.*

42   12step.org is a resource for all things related to; the 12-step program, *http://www.12step.org/the-12-steps/step-2/*; changed to use inclusive language.

43   http://www.12step.org/the-12-steps/step-2/.

44   Richard Middleton, "After *The Liberating Image*," on the website *Jesus Creed*, http://www.patheos.com/blogs /jesuscreed/2014/08/05/richard-middleton-after-the-liberating-image-rjs/.

45 Ibid.

46 Tal Ben-Shahar, *Happier: Learn the Secrets to Daily Joy and Lasting Fulfillment*, Kindle edition (New York: McGraw-Hill Education, 2007), 20–21.

47 Shawn Achor, *The Happiness Advantage: The Seven Principles of Positive Psychology That Fuel Success and Performance at Work*, Kindle edition (New York: Crown Business, 2010), 92.

48 Gregory Boyle, *Tattoos on the Heart: The Power of Boundless Compassion*, Kindle edition (New York: Free Press, 2010), 50.

49 Achor, *The Happiness Advantage,* 101.

50 Seligman, *Flourish,* Kindle location 4855.

51 Achor, *The Happiness Advantage,* 97–98.

52 Oliver Sacks, "To See and Not See," *The New Yorker* (May 10, 1993), 59.

53 See G. C. Berkouwer, *The Triumph of Grace in the Theology of Karl Barth* (Grand Rapids: Wm. B. Eerdmans Publishing Co., 1956).

54 On Francis and the Franciscans, see Johannes Fried and Peter Lewis, *The Middle Ages* (New York: Belknap Press, 2015).

55 There is voluminous literature on Wesley and the rise of Methodism. See, for instance, Ronald H. Stone, *John Wesley's Life and Ethics* (Nashville: Abingdon, 2001); also Richard P. Heitzenrater, *Wesley and the People Called Methodists*, Second edition (Nashville: Abingdon, 2013).

56 Bill Lohmann, "Spiritual independence a growing trend," *Richmond Times-Dispatch* (April 25, 2015).

57 See *www.christchurchcharlotte.org*

58 Fowler, *Stages of Faith.*

59 Ken Gire, *Answering the Call: The Doctor Who Made Africa His Life: The Remarkable Story of Albert Schweitzer* (Nashville: Thomas Nelson, 2013).

60 David Gregory, *How's Your Faith? An Unlikely Spiritual Journey* (New York: Simon & Schuster, 2015).

61 A fascinating account of Loyola, the Exercises, and the Jesuits is found in Chris Lowney, *Heroic Leadership: Best Practices from a 450-Year-Old Company That Changed the World* (Chicago: Loyola Press, 2005).

62 Borg details his own intellectual and faith development in *Convictions: How I Learned What Matters Most* (New York: HarperOne, 2014). This book reiterates his conclusions in an earlier volume, *The God We Never Knew: Beyond Dogmatic Religion to a More Authentic Contemporary Faith* (New York: HarperOne, 1998).

63 See David Bentley Hart, *Atheist Delusions: The Christian Revolution and Its Fashionable Enemies* (New Haven: Yale University Press, 2010).

64 Daniel C. Maguire, *Christianity without God: Moving beyond the Dogmas and Retrieving the Epic Moral Narrative* (Albany: SUNY Press, 2014); Ronald Dworkin, *Religion without God* (New York: Harvard University Press, 2013).

65 Lisa Miller, *The Spiritual Child: The New Science on Parenting for Health and Lifelong Thriving* (New York: St. Martin's Press, 2015).

Select Bibliography

Achor, Shawn. *The Happiness Advantage: The Seven Principles of Positive Psychology That Fuel Success and Performance at Work.* Kindle edition. New York: Crown Publishing Group, 2010.

Aitken, Jonathan. *John Newton: From Disgrace to Amazing Grace.* Wheaton, IL: Crossway, 2013.

Augustine. *The Confessions.* Translated by Henry Chadwick. Book X, Chapter 8. Oxford: Oxford University Press: 2009.

Ben-Shahar, Tal. *Happier: Learn the Secrets to Daily Joy and Lasting Fulfillment.* Kindle edition. New York: McGraw-Hill, 2007.

Berkouwer, G. C. *The Triumph of Grace in the Theology of Karl Barth.* Grand Rapids: Wm. B. Eerdmans Publishing Co., 1956.

Borg, Marcus. *The God We Never Knew: Beyond Dogmatic Religion to a More Authentic Contemporary Faith.* New York: HarperOne, 1998.

———. *Convictions: How I Learned What Matters Most.* New York: HarperOne, 2014.

Bregman, Lucy. *The Ecology of Spirituality: Meanings, Virtues, and Practices in a Post-Religious Age.* Kindle edition. Waco, TX: Baylor University Press, 2014.

Brooks, David. "The Subtle Sensations of Faith." *New York Times*, December 22, 2014.

Brown, Brené. *I Thought It Was Just Me (but It Isn't): Making the Journey from "What Will People Think?" to "I Am Enough."* New York: Avery, 2007.

Boyle, Gregory. *Tattoos on the Heart: The Power of Boundless Compassion.* Kindle edition. New York: Free Press, 2010.

Christian, William A., Jr. *Visionaries: The Spanish Republic and the Reign of Christ.* Oakland: University of California Press, 1996.

Dworkin, Ronald. *Religion without God.* New York: Harvard University Press, 2013.

Eliade, Mircea. *The History of Religious Ideas, Volume 3: From Muhammad to the Age of Reforms.* Translated by Alf Hiltebeitel. Chicago: University of Chicago, 1988.

Eliot, T. S. *Collected Poems, 1909-1962.* San Diego: Harcourt Brace Jovanovich, 1991.

Fields, Alison and Robert Kominski. "America: A Nation on the Move." *United States Census Bureau,* December 10, 2012, http://blogs.census.gov/2012/12/10/america-a-nation-on-the-move/.

Fowler, James. *Stages of Faith: The Psychology of Human Development and the Quest for Meaning.* New York: HarperCollins, 1995.

Fried, Johannes, and Peter Lewis, *The Middle Ages.* New York: Belknap Press, 2015.

Gire, Ken. *Answering the Call: The Doctor Who Made Africa His Life: The Remarkable Story of Albert Schweitzer.* Nashville: Thomas Nelson, 2013.

Gregory, David. *How's Your Faith? An Unlikely Spiritual Journey.* New York: Simon & Schuster, 2015.

Haidt, Jonathan. *The Happiness Hypothesis: Finding Modern Truth in Ancient Wisdom.* Kindle edition. New York: Basic Books, 2006.

Hart, David Bentley. *Atheist Delusions: The Christian Revolution and Its Fashionable Enemies.* New Haven, CT: Yale University Press, 2010.

Heitzenrater, Richard P. *Wesley and the People Called Methodists.* 2nd edition. Nashville, TN: Abingdon, 2013.

Hunter, James Davison. *To Change the World: The Irony, Tragedy, and Possibility of Christianity in the Late Modern World.* Kindle edition. Oxford: Oxford University Press, 2010.

Junger, Sebastian. *The Perfect Storm.* New York: W. W. Norton & Company, Inc., 1997.

Kirn, Walter. *Up in the Air.* New York: Anchor, 2002.

Kubler-Ross, Elisabeth. *On Death and Dying: What the Dying Have to Teach Doctors, Nurses, Clergy and Their Own Families.* New York: Scribner, 2014.

Lewis, Meriwether, and William Clark. *The Journals of Lewis and Clark.* New York: Mariner Books, 1997.

Lohmann, Bill. "Spiritual Independence a Growing Trend." *Richmond Times-Dispatch,* April 25, 2015.

Lowney, Chris. *Heroic Leadership: Best Practices from a 450-Year-Old Company That Changed the World.* Chicago: Loyola Press, 2005.

Maguire, Daniel C. *Christianity without God: Moving beyond the Dogmas and Retrieving the Epic Moral Narrative.* Albany: SUNY Press, 2014.

McLaren, Brian. "A Reading of John 14:6." http://www.brianmclaren.net/emc/archives/McLaren%20-%20John%2014.6.pdf.

Middleton, Richard. "After *The Liberating Image.*" *Jesus Creed.* http://www.patheos.com/blogs/jesuscreed/2014/08/05/richard-middleton-after-the-liberating-image-rjs/.

Miller, Lisa. *The Spiritual Child: The New Science on Parenting for Health and Lifelong Thriving.* New York: St. Martin's Press, 2015.

Pew Research Center. "Millennials: Confident. Connected. Open to Change." February 24, 2010, http://www.pewsocialtrends.org/2010/02/24/millennials-confident-connected-open-to-change/.

———. "America's Changing Religious Landscape." May 12, 2015, http://www.pewforum.org/2015/05/12/americas-changing-religious-landscape/.

Peterson, Eugene H. *The Pastor: A Memoir*. Kindle edition. New York: HarperOne, 2011.

Sacks, Oliver. "To See and Not See." *New Yorker*, May 10, 1993.

———. *Hallucinations*. New York: Vintage, 2013.

Schwartz, Barry. *The Paradox of Choice: Why More Is Less*. New York: Harper Perennial, 2005.

Scruton, Roger. *The Face of God: The Gifford Lectures*. New York: Bloomsbury Academic, 2012.

———. *The Soul of the World*. Princeton, NJ: Princeton University Press, 2014.

Seligman, Martin. *Flourish: A Visionary New Understanding of Happiness and Well-Being*. Kindle edition. New York: Free Press, 2011.

Southey, Robert. *Common-place Book*. 1850. London: Forgotten Books, 2015.

Strayed, Cheryl. *Wild: From Lost to Found on the Pacific Coast Trail*. New York: Vintage, 2013.

Stone, Ronald H. *John Wesley's Life and Ethics*. Nashville, TN: Abingdon, 2001.

Sullivan, Amy. "Church Shopping: Why Americans Change Faiths." *Time*. April 28, 2009., http://content.time.com/time/nation/article/0,8599,1894361,00.html.

Taves, Ann. *Fits, Trances and Visions: Experiencing Religion and Explaining Experience from Wesley to James*. Princeton, NJ: Princeton University Press, 1999.

Thoreau, Henry David. *Walden*. New York: Empire Books, 2013.

Towns, Eleni. "The 9/11 Generation: How 9/11 Shaped the Millennial Generation." *Center for American Progress*, September 8, 2011. https://www.americanprogress.org/issues/religion/news/2011/09/08/10363/the-911-generation/.

CPSIA information can be obtained
at www.ICGtesting.com
Printed in the USA
FSOW01n2115080916
24792FS